D0772319

BLACK
IS THE NEW
WHITE

PAUL MOONEY

BLACK
IS THE NEW
WHITE

A MEMOIR

SIMON SPOTLIGHT ENTERTAINMENT

NEW YORK   LONDON   TORONTO   SYDNEY

Simon Spotlight Entertainment
A Division of Simon & Schuster, Inc.
1230 Avenue of the Americas
New York, NY 10020

First Simon Spotlight Entertainment hardcover edition November 2009

SIMON SPOTLIGHT ENTERTAINMENT and colophon are trademarks of
Simon & Schuster, Inc.

For information about special discounts for bulk purchases, please contact
Simon & Schuster Special Sales at 1-866-506-1949 or business@
simonandschuster.com.

The Simon & Schuster Speakers Bureau can bring authors to your
live event. For more information or to book an event contact the Simon
& Schuster Speakers Bureau at 1-866-248-3049 or visit our website
at www.simonspeakers.com.

Designed by Jaime Putorti

Manufactured in the United States of America

10 9 8 7 6 5 4 3 2 1

Library of Congress Cataloging-in-Publication Data

Mooney, Paul
   Black is the new white / by Paul Mooney.
      p. cm.
      1. Mooney, Paul, 1941– 2. Television comedy writers—United States—
Biography. 3. African American comedians—Biography. I. Title.
   PN1992.4.M66 2009
   792.702'8092—dc22   2009019572

ISBN 978-1-4165-8795-8
ISBN 978-1-4169-6853-5 (ebook)

To my beloved Mama

FOREWORD
BY DAVE CHAPPELLE

When I was a young black boy growing up in Washington, D.C., during my formative years, my comic inspiration came from various comedy idols, particularly Richard Pryor and Eddie Murphy.

Richard meant so much to me. Richard Pryor was the real King of Comedy. Then I found out that Paul Mooney was the writer behind my idol!

We all remember that famous sketch from *Saturday Night Live*'s first season, where Pryor plays a prospective employee playing a "word association game" with the interviewer (played by Chevy Chase). The two get into a verbal fight when Chase's character begins to use racial slurs.

Well, Paul Mooney wrote that sketch!

To see a black man on TV, holding his own with a white man, that was television history. It changed everything, not only TV, but also my course, and it gave me the direction my life was meant to go in.

The Eddie Murphy Raw tour in the 1980s was the hottest ticket in town. When the fans came in wanting to see Eddie Murphy, for the first half of the show, they got Paul Mooney.

I thought, *That nigga had a lot of balls to open up for a crowd that was only there to see Eddie Murphy.*

Years later, I asked Eddie about it: "Why did you put Paul Mooney on to open for you?"

"When you have Paul Mooney in front of you," Eddie said, "you have to be on the top of your game when you come out to perform. You can't slack if Mooney is the opening act."

I had the good fortune to work with Paul on *Chappelle's Show* and I have some stories of my own. Paul Mooney is a genius, brilliant, a legend, and a force to be reckoned with.

But I will say this: you don't fuck with Paul Mooney, you don't fuck with his writing, his material, his sketches . . . and you certainly *don't tell him what to do!* Trust me, I've learned, especially when I worked with him on my own show.

When I started gearing up for my show, I knew I needed Paul Mooney to be part of it. I just wanted his comedic genius. I wanted to be around someone who has so much history and success. Mooney was the writer, the casting director, and the director for some segments of *The Richard Pryor Show* in 1977 for NBC.

That was classic television, never to be duplicated. Working on *The Richard Pryor Show,* Paul Mooney helped launch the careers of so many talented comedians and actors: Robin Williams, Brad Garrett, Shirley Hemphill, Marsha Warfield, Johnny Witherspoon, Tim Reid, and Sandra Bernhard, to name a few.

There are a lot of things people remember about my show. Some things that *I* did, yeah, but a lot of people remember "Negrodamus" and "Ask a Black Dude." It was classic Mooney.

Now, many of you reading this book may not have even heard of Paul Mooney, and that's a shame. Why isn't Mooney a mainstream star? As you read through the pages you will find out why . . . Paul Mooney was *too black for Hollywood!*

Say what you will about Paul Mooney, he always delivers the goods. What comes out of his mind is comic genius at its best.

Paul Mooney: the face that launched a thousand quips

RICHARD

CHAPTER 1

I'm sliding into a booth in a coffee shop on Santa Monica Boulevard, slapping the table to wake Richard Pryor from his hangover nod.

"Man," I say to him, "I just saw a lady so pretty, somebody should suck her daddy's dick for a job well done."

Richard stares at me. Early afternoon, too early for Richard. I smell the brandy he doses his coffee with. He is a little slowed-down by all the poisons in his blood, but even slowed-down Richard Pryor is quicker than any other human being on earth.

He laughs. I'm not saying Richard just laughs like an ordinary person laughs. I mean he *laughs*. His face lights up like a Times Square billboard and his whole body wags like a dog happy to see its owner.

You know you can die happy when you can make Richard Pryor laugh. It's this huge blast of appreciation, hipness, and intelligence. He *gets* it. His laugh is like ripping open a bag of joy, letting loose a storm that blows you head over heels. It is that powerful.

The greatest comics—and Richard is bar none *the* greatest—always have the greatest laughs.

Later on, as the hard living takes its toll and the MS takes over, most of Richard's laughs will turn into fits of coughing, as though he's trying to hack up his liver. But a Richard Pryor laugh is still and always will be like getting a high five from God.

California yellow sun and Pacific blue sky. That September day in 1968, Richard and I are in Duke's Coffee Shop, the original one, in the old Tropicana Motel. *Two dudes, two dudes,* like Richard starts one of his routines. We are the only black guys who can make the scene in Hollywood. We are groundbreakers, accepted at all the clubs, invited to all the parties. When we break into it, Hollywood is still a closed, racist town. The place has never seen anybody like us. We are fearless. We go everywhere. We break down barriers. We still get harassed by bigots and cheated by the system, but it never stops us.

Later that night my wife, Yvonne, gets dressed up and we go to Troubadour on Santa Monica to hear Richard perform his stand-up routine. He's a different comic when I am in the audience. He hears my laugh and he shifts gears, elevating his act to a higher, edgier level. I can tell he is trying to make me laugh, but I'm not going to give it up that easy. I make him work for it. He pushes himself.

From the stage of the Troub that night, I hear Richard do the line I gave him earlier in Duke's coffee shop.

"Coming here tonight, I saw a woman so motherfucking beautiful gorgeous that it made me want to suck her daddy's dick for a job well done."

The joke *kills.* The way Richard tells it, it *kills.* The audience practically vomits laughter.

Later that same night—or is it early morning by then?—Richard tells me to hold my arm out.

"What for?"

"Just hold it out, motherfucker."

He slips a watch on my wrist. A good watch—I can feel its heavyweight mass on my arm—a $10,000 beauty. The kind of watch you call a *timepiece*.

"What's this for?"

"The bit," he says.

"What bit?" I play dumb.

"The suck-her-father's-dick bit."

"Oh, that," I say. "That's just you and me talking. I could hardly tell if you were awake when I told you that."

"Take the fucking watch. You don't like it, motherfucker, sell it. Take the money, Mr. Mooney."

He always calls me that. Mr. Mooney. Off that character on the *The Lucy Show*.

I take the watch.

The funniest man on the face of the earth wants me to write for him. It begins to click. I think: This thing we have, this Batman-and-Robin thing, can somehow turn into something that means money and good times for both of us. I toss lines to Richard. He puts them out to the audience. The audience flings money at him. Richard throws money at me.

The truth is, it's never about the money for me. I love Richard. I am his biggest fan. I get off on him doing one of my jokes. It means so much to me. I want Richard to be happy and to succeed. My loyalty is to Richard, and my relationship with him is authentic, as though he is my brother. On all of Richard's albums, you can hear me laugh. I always laugh long and loud.

Those first days together in 1968 are the beginning of a beautiful friendship.

CHAPTER 2

First time I meet Richard Pryor, it's in the late 1960s at a crowded party in my bungalow on Sunset. The place is full of people.

Richard walks in, and right away I sense he is different. Out of the corner of my eye, I chart his course through the party people. He has a woman with him, but she trails behind as though he has forgotten all about her.

He is smiling and laughing. Everything pleases him. He knows there are lots of women and drugs around, and that fills him with childish delight.

Like a kid in a candy store, I think.

He is the eternal child. That is Richard's whole secret, right there. A lot of us swallow our childlike side, beat it down, scorch it clean. Not Richard. He speaks with the vulnerability of a child, and that's what makes people love him.

So he makes his way through the party, and finally he arrives at me, and right away, the first thing out of his mouth, he says he wants to go to bed with me.

Not me, personally. Ain't nobody straighter and more pussy-crazy than Richard. He means he wants to go to bed with me and the women I am with and the woman he's with and whatever other women he can convince to jump in with us. All of us together.

"Let's all get in bed and have a freak thing!" he says.

The first words I ever hear out of Richard Pryor's mouth.

Only, the woman I am with is my half sister, Carol LaBrea. Carol is drop-dead gorgeous. She's a model, the first black woman ever to make it on the cover of a white fashion magazine, French *Vogue*. Naturally, Richard is knocked out by her.

Carol knows the woman Richard's with, a cute little girl who works for pro football Hall of Famer and actor Jim Brown. Carol and she moonlight as go-go dancers in the cages at Whisky A Go Go on the Strip.

Hollywood, 1968. Everyone in town is talking about a new movie being shot at Columbia Pictures. A free-love kind of movie. *Bob & Carol & Ted & Alice* it's called when it comes out, but right now everyone refers to it as "the Natalie Wood swingers movie." Or "Elliot Gould's thing where he winds up in bed with everybody."

I always call it *Bob & Carol & Ted & Lassie*.

Orgies are in the air back then.

I look at Richard, and I'm thinking, *Who is this freak?*

I laugh and say, "You just say whatever comes into your head, don't you?"

Richard laughs. "Let's go, let's do it, man, look at these ladies!"

Who is this . . . *child*? Because that's how he strikes me right away. A lot of people might come out of the bag at him, get all pissed because he's suggesting an orgy. I have all the more reason to be affronted, since Carol is my half sister.

But from the very start, from that first meeting, I find it impossible to get angry at Richard. He's so obviously without guile. He just has no inhibitions. Like a baby—*I want the tit, and I am going to grab for the tit.*

No other considerations figure into his actions, nothing else other than "I want it." No ideas like, Well, this might not be cool, or, maybe I'm being rude—nothing like that. The man is short on impulse control.

For everybody else in the world, an attitude such as this comes off as totally insufferable. But Richard makes it work because he's completely open and vulnerable. Sure, he's selfish. But he's selfish with the innocence of a four-year-old. He's like the way I used to be when I was a child. He makes me feel protective toward him.

I tell him no, I am not going to get into an orgy with him.

Richard slides away from me like the iceberg sliding away from the *Titanic.* I watch him as he continues on, crashing into other groups and couples at the party. *Wanna do an orgy?* I have to laugh. I don't feel any blowback or negativity from him because I refuse. He just moves on to the next possibility. But that brief run-in gives me a strange gut feeling, as though everything in my world is going to change.

"If he keeps that up," Carol says, "he's going to get himself a beatdown."

"If he keeps that up," I say, "he's going to get himself laid."

Two weeks later, I bump into him again at a Trini Lopez concert in West Hollywood. I see him at the after-party backstage, and he runs around pretending to hide from me. When I finally corner him, he fake cowers and says, "Don't hit me!" I can't help laughing.

"If I'd a known she was your sister, I never would have said that," Richard says.

"How'd you do that night?" I ask him. "You ever find an orgy?"

"Oh, I did okay," he says, laughing. But not before I catch something vague about his response.

"You don't remember what happened that night, do you?" I say.

"I must've been high," he says. He shrugs.

It's the first hint I get of Richard Pryor's Eternal Present. *Maybe I should just fade away from him right now,* I think. *Avoid a lot of trouble.* Then Richard laughs, and I know I'm hooked. We have a drink together, and just like that, we are best friends. It's as though I have known him all my life. It's that deep, that quick.

Even though I have a feeling that sooner or later it's all going to crash, I still accept Richard's friendship. He is irresistible.

CHAPTER 3

In 1968, Richard has one foot in the straight world and one foot hovering in midair. He's in the process of stepping forward into a new style of comedy of his own making, but he's still wondering how it's going to play onstage. He's off balance.

Bill Cosby represents straight success, straight comedy, straight laughs. He is monster, the most successful comic of the day. Hit albums, riffs that are being copied in every schoolyard in the country, kids acting them out line by line. Funny, funny shit.

For white people, Bill is the perfect Negro. He's the Sidney Poitier of comedy, very clean-cut and articulate. White folks love to use that word to describe us. *Articulate*. It means we don't grunt like jungle savages.

Richard thinks he wants to be Bill Cosby. For a long time, that's what he goes for. Richard is talented in so many ways that he can do it, too. He does a physical-comedy routine where he imitates a bowling pin waiting to be knocked down by a ball coming down the alley. He flinches because the pin boy's hands are cold. He dodges and wobbles and finally remains standing.

Cosby would be comfortable doing that routine. He wouldn't do it as well as Richard, but it's in his wheelhouse.

Pryor-doing-Cosby is pretty successful. Ed Sullivan has him on the show. Richard does his act in prime venues all over the country. He plays Vegas. It's all starting to rain down on him—the money, the women, the fame.

So Richard has one foot in Cosbyland. But there's something inside him that knows it's not quite right. He wants to do something else, something truer to his experience.

Richard doesn't fucking bowl. He doesn't hang out in bowling alleys. Pin boys are vanishing, replaced by automatic pinsetters. So why is he doing a routine about bowling? He's trying to please people.

That's where comedy is back then. It skates on the surface. It makes the audience members laugh but doesn't give them anything heavy-duty to take home. Going for the laugh is fine, but going for the laugh and the thought and the emotion all at the same time is better. Richard is taking a step in that direction, and so am I.

When I see Richard's act, I think it's all right. Not great. Just all right. I laugh. I know that somewhere underneath all the bullshit, he's a natural. But what he's doing doesn't hit me in the heart. It doesn't hit Richard in the heart, either, and that's part of the problem. He's a kid in a candy store who is craving steak. He can get the sugar-sweet laughs easy enough, but he wants something more substantial.

And the only way to do something more substantial on-stage—then and now—is to discuss one of the defining features of the American experience: race. I don't know how anyone, black or white, in America can stand up in front of an audience with a microphone and never mention it. It's as if there's an elephant in the room, and it's spraying out elephant diarrhea all over everyone, and no one's mentioning it. It's surreal.

My impulse is always to call people's attention to the situation. *Uh, the elephant? Shitting on you?*

I never hear Richard's comedy god Bill Cosby make a race-based joke or observation in his act. Before my time, when he's just starting out, he tries race-based humor, but gives it up. He attempts the impossible: racial neutrality.

Offstage, Cosby does talk about race. "If you're really going to do a show about the black family," he says, talking about his obsession, the TV sitcom, "you're going to have to bring out the heavy. And who is the heavy but the white bigot? This would be very painful for most whites to see."

Years later, in 1984, when Cosby does a popular sitcom about the black family, he doesn't "bring out the white bigot" at all. *The Cosby Show* is like a race-free zone. I don't get it. Why the disconnect? Because nobody wants to rock the boat. No one wants to disturb the white audience.

I don't believe in racial neutrality. It's always a lie. White comics can ignore race because they've been trained their whole lives to turn a blind eye to the big, loose-boweled elephant. That's what white people do. They only bring up race when it suits their purposes.

Black comics have a "double consciousness," in the way W. E. B. DuBois uses the phrase, meaning they have one self for the master and one self that's "just between us." Back in the sixties and seventies, when I first hit the scene, the stage is definitely the master's territory. If they want to gain a wide crossover audience, black comics have to be careful what they say.

But that's not me. I don't have a double consciousness. I am who I am. I'm the first comic to bring a "just between us" black voice to the stage, to any stage, any audience, white, black, or mixed. I'm not a different person onstage and off, like Cosby used to be. I don't do one act in South Central and another on the Strip, the way Redd Foxx used to do.

Fuck that shit. I keep it real.

Richard plays the middle, too—until the effert of trying to balance voices and audiences makes his head explode on-stage. It's a legendary incident in stand-up comedy. He is at the Aladdin, with Dean Martin in the audience. He's doing his Bill Cosby–Ed Sullivan routines. Surefire laugh-getters.

And suddenly he stops. He stares out at the audience. He has a slow-motion breakdown. The gap between what he's saying and what he's feeling is just too huge.

"What the fuck am I doing here?" he says, and he walks offstage.

His meltdown is already a year in his past when I start hanging with him. Richard likes to think that the Aladdin moment is an epiphany. That's how he describes it to me. He wants it to be clear-cut, as though there is a before and an after, the "hi-ya-Dean-o!" Aladdin Richard, and then the cooler, hipper, realer post-Aladdin Richard.

But when I meet him, the changeover is still nowhere near complete. He's still channeling Cosby. He's still unhappy with himself.

"I was thinking about Mama," he says, when I ask him about what happened that night at the Aladdin.

Richard and I both have grandmothers we call Mama. It's one of the things we have in common that bonds us. My mama is my mother's mother, Aimay Ealy. Richard's mama, Marie Bryant, is a tough-as-nails brothel keeper in Peoria, Illinois.

"I was looking out at the audience," Richard says, "and it hit me that all those motherfuckers out there wouldn't make room for Mama if you put a gun to their heads."

No room for Richard's Mama in the audience, and no room for the real Richard behind the microphone. That's why he says "fuck it" and walks away.

But total transformation isn't so easy. He can't just snap his fingers and make it happen. One of the reasons why he gloms onto me, I know, is that he sees something in the way I carry myself that he wants to emulate.

"Thing about you, Mooney," he says, "you don't give a shit. You ain't scared of white people."

He laughs like the idea tickles him.

It's true. Whatever the quality is that white people enjoy in black people, I ain't got it.

Or maybe it's a question of what I do have—my self-assurance. I try to keep it real, I always have. But not many white people like it "real."

It's as though when black people's hair is relaxed, white people are relaxed. When it's nappy, they're not happy. And I have a nappy mental attitude.

Richard brings me to a small party in Venice, near the beach. I see right away that it's not my scene. Dope smoke in the air. Cocaine on the table. It's my nightmare in the flesh. I've been at enough parties like this to know that I hate them. Sometimes it seems like everyone in L.A. is high but me.

"Hey, man," I say to Richard. "I'm going to cut out." I head for the door.

"Mooney!" Richard comes after me. "What's the matter?"

"I got to go."

"We just got here!"

"You do what you want. It's just not the kind of scene I'm into."

"No blow?" Richard stares. "You don't smoke dope, either?"

"And I don't drink. Not the kind of drinking that's going on around here."

"Motherfucker," Richard says, shaking his head, baffled.

It's difficult for him to comprehend. "Are you a motherfucking Mormon?"

"I'll see you later."

He gets a hurt, childlike look on his face because I am rejecting him. Then his face brightens. "Hey, you know what? Come back, we'll hang out."

He grabs my arm and physically ushers me back into the living room.

"Mr. Mooney's cool," he announces. "He is keeping it straight. Mr. Mooney doesn't do none of this shit."

Everyone's staring at me. "That's okay, that's okay," Richard says, sitting down and pulling a mirror toward him that has a half dozen rails laid out on it.

"I get Paul's share," he says, snorting a generous noseful. "More for me."

He cackles.

I hear that same line again and again during the whole time I know Richard. "I get Mooney's share," he says gleefully. I'm his shadow partner. I automatically double his drug intake.

The Venice party is like a fork in the road for me. Decision time. I can back away with a "Thanks, but no thanks." I can leave the dope room, like I usually do. Or I can stay.

I stay. I slide into the role. I'm the only straight person in the whole crowd that flocks around Richard. I'm the one who can find the car. I'm the one who remembers what street the party's on. I'm the one who doesn't get us lost.

As Richard's shadow partner, I witness more drugs being smoked, snorted, and swallowed than any other straight person on the face of the earth. It doesn't bother me. If it bothers anyone else, Richard makes it right.

"It's cool, real cool," he says, laughing, elbowing his way to bend over the coffee table trough. "I get Mooney's share!"

At the Venice party, I get that kid-in-the-candy-store vibe again. There's something desperate about Richard stuffing his face with dope and drink. Something is bothering him, something deep down at the root of his soul.

Richard has to get out more, I think. A pretty funny thought, since all Richard seems to do is go out and party. I decide to push him a little bit. Or maybe just lead and let him follow.

Two dudes: Richard Pryor and me out on the town

CHAPTER 4

On the club scene in Los Angeles in the late sixties, the main turf for comics is the Strip—the section of Sunset Boulevard that's now incorporated as West Hollywood but back then is still wild and lawless Los Angeles County. It's patrolled not by the Gestapo LAPD but by the more lax L.A. County Sheriff's deputies.

On the Strip, comics open for rock acts at Whisky A Go Go, Bido Lito's, the Trip, or Ciro's, and do sets at the Fifth Estate, the Stratford Hotel, or Troubadour, just down the hill on Santa Monica Boulevard.

But there's a whole different scene that happens a long way away from Sunset Boulevard. Down on Crenshaw and in South Central, a few clubs bring in black audiences and feature the kind of comedy that nobody is ready for on the Strip. Not coon comedy, not clowning, but comedy that talks about what is going on in front of everyone's faces and no one usually dares to mention onstage.

Redd Foxx has his own club a few blocks south of the freeway, Jazz Go-Go, on Adams off Western. He mixes stand-up, music, and strippers. He's got another club on La Cienega, which is named after him. Richard idolizes Redd. He is the true groundbreaker. In a lot of ways, he is the anti-Cosby.

We all cut our teeth on Redd's party albums, like *You Gotta Wash Your Ass!* They're blue, blue, blue, but funny, funny, funny. In his clubs he's always introduced with the line "The two funniest four-letter words in the English language—Redd Foxx!" He never holds back on the street talk.

> *Yeah, I said the word* shit. *I said "shit" not to shock anyone but because I'm too old to stand up here and say "doo-doo." If you tell the truth, you know you say "shit," too. If you ain't said "shit" before, come out in the parking lot with me, and let me slam the car door on your hand. You'll say "shit" and "motherfucker" both. Shit! Motherfucker!*

When idiots ask Richard why he drops the *M* word so much, he says that it's because America slammed the car door on his hand. Nobody knows what he means when he says that, but I remember Redd's riff and I laugh.

Farther south on Crenshaw is another club, Maverick's Flat. John Daniels takes an old Arthur Murray dancing school and decorates it in late-1960's-style funk. Fluffy sofas, glass-tile tabletops, freaky *Bitches Brew* paintings a couple of years before Miles ever comes out with his album *Bitches Brew.*

The Temptations open the place in January 1966, and later come out with a song about it, "Psychedelic Shack." "Psychedelic shack, that's where it's at . . . I guarantee you this place will blow your mind."

The football great Jim Brown backs Daniels with money and with his celebrity juice. Jim Brown is like the Great Black Hope. He's everywhere. He does so much for the community. He takes care of children, he counsels dropouts, he pumps money into businesses.

Pretty soon after Richard and I start going to Maverick's Flat, it blows up big. White hipsters like Steve McQueen and Marlon Brando are showing up. It becomes a favorite place for them to slum. The comic Flip Wilson is around, too, just on the cusp of getting his own TV variety show.

Richard is a little dubious about Maverick's at first because Daniels runs the place as a private club and serves no liquor, only ice-cold Coca-Cola. But soon enough Richard realizes that he can easily get from other clubgoers a supply of his three major food groups: booze, cocaine, pussy.

Maverick's is open late, after the clubs on the Strip close at 2 a.m. I like the place because of its dance floor. Deep down I think of myself first as a dancer. There is a silhouetted Arthur Murray logo embedded in the floor at Maverick's entrance, and I always tap it with my foot for good luck as I head inside.

Richard can't dance worth shit. But John Daniels likes him. "I can't dance, but I can *move*," Richard says, doing some sort of pimp strut-roll that makes everyone laugh.

At those Crenshaw clubs, Maverick's and Redd Foxx's, I watch a snake shimmy out of its skin—or maybe a butterfly come out of its chrysalis. Richard leaves behind his Bill Cosby–style routines and begins fumbling around for his new voice. Daniels hires him to do a few shows. Redd Foxx gives him a microphone any time he wants it.

One night, Richard puts on an outrageous character I instantly recognize from my childhood. It's the kind of pompous, self-inflated preacher every black churchgoer knows.

"I first met God in 1929," Richard says, drawing out the year with a flourish straight from the pulpit. "Twenty-naaaahn."

I'm walking down the street, eating a sandwich, and I hear a magnificent voice calling to me out of a dark alleyway. I recognize the voice of God right away, since it is deep and glorious and sounds sacred. But I don't go down into that dark alley, in case there were three niggers down there waiting for me with baseball bats.

A-men, reverend. It feels right. I hear the true voice of the preacher in the bit, and the familiar street wisdom so common in the ghetto. It helps that I'm out there in the audience. Richard hears my laugh and it eggs him on.

I realize that he's doing something different. He's not doing jokes so much anymore. I'm still feeding him laugh lines, and they still pop up in his act. But he's moving beyond that now. Jokes are Cosbyland to him.

He's beginning to do characters, situations, street arguments, weird-shit human behavior.

Comics are like trapeze artists—some can't work without a net, some can't work with one. Comics like George Carlin are crafting every line, every pause. It's funny, but it's all completely canned. When Richard gets up onstage at Maverick's, he never knows what he's going to say. The words just spill out.

I've done enough improv to know how tough it is to do what Richard's doing. Just a man and a microphone, saying whatever's on his mind at that moment, developing it on the spot into a routine. It's the purest kind of improvisation, and Richard proves himself brilliant at it. Every night is different. Richard plays off the audience. If they're with him, he rises to meet them. If they're cold, he's cold.

Richard's favorite word is *motherfucker*. Richard loves him some "motherfuckers" in his act. I always joke with him that I am going to get my own mama to go on TV with a lobbying campaign against the "*M*-word."

His second favorite word at Maverick's and Redd's is *nigger*. When he's up onstage, he speaks what he hears on the streets, at parties, and during drug transactions. What Richard does is knock down the walls between who he is onstage and who he is off it, until there's less and less of a difference between the two.

His routines are no longer comic confections whipped up in some comedy kitchen. They come straight out of his bent life.

Sitting in Maverick's, listening to Richard's new routines, I think, *My God, he's left jokes behind*. Then I think, *Am I in trouble? Is he going to leave me behind, too?*

CHAPTER 5

I love jokes. I love gags. I love punch lines. That's who I am.

I know this puts me totally out of step with the times. Every stand-up comic in the universe nowadays runs away from jokes like they are the Black Plague. (Why was the plague black? Didn't it kill mostly white people? Shouldn't it be called the White Plague?) Jokes are old-fashioned. Comics do *situations* now. But I love jokes because they're street.

Tell a joke, and if it's a good joke, it turns into a virus. Spreads faster than a flu. If there actually ever is a real Killer Joke, we'll all be dead. It'll hit us quicker than a jab from Ali's right hand.

Walking down One-Two-Five in Harlem, corner of Lenox, I hear a street peddler tell a joke to a B.I.D. lady. I keep walking, and before I get two blocks, I hear a stumble-bum tell the same joke to a little audience of hustlers outside the Uptown Wine Pantry near Madison. Punch lines travel quicker than I can walk.

Jokes are the original Internet. They connect people.

Jokes travel through time, too. A joke dies and it lies

there asleep and then someone comes along and spills water on it and it comes alive again.

The original joke is all God's. It's the gag he's playing on each and every one of us. It's called life. God's joke is the funniest of all. An oldie but goodie. The Big Bang is the Big Punch Line.

A joke once freed a slave. This is true. Master is moaning to his house servant, "I'm so homely, I'm so homely, my face could crack a sink. No woman will look at me. I go out, I scare the horses."

Slave shakes his head in sympathy and keeps on sweeping the parlor floor. "I know what you can do," slave says.

"You do?" says the master, overjoyed. "Tell me!"

Slave smiles, shakes his head, and sweeps.

"You tell me the answer," Master says, "I'll free you right away."

That perks the slave up and makes him stop his broom.

"Tell me," Master pleads. "How can I stop this homely face of mine from scaring people?"

"All right, I'll tell you—you can keep your ugly ass at home!"

Comedians don't tell jokes. Not anymore. The only people who tell jokes are me and police and sanit-men and salesmen and B.I.D. ladies and long-haul truckers and nurses and exterminators and stumble-bums and addicts and jet-jocks and golfers and car mechanics and frat boys and children.

Children tell jokes. We've got to listen to the children.

A seven-year-old comes into her parents' bedroom with her little six-year-old friend. Her mom and dad are in bed, and they're tearing it up, Mom giving Dad head like she's Monica and he's Bill. Hoovering it down like she could suck the chrome off a hubcap.

Seven-year-old turns to her friend and says, "Can you believe it? And they give me an ass-whipping for sucking my thumb!"

Listen to the children. *Listen to the children!*

Twelve-year-old kid goes into his parents' bedroom and sees his mom and dad really going at it. Dad's got Mom spread-eagled and he's pounding her like a pile driver. Dad looks over his shoulder and sees the kid and laughs. Heh, heh, heh. *Haw!*

A month later the dad comes into the kid's bedroom, the kid's got Grandma spread-eagled and he's really giving it to her, wailing away. Dad freaks out. Kid looks over his shoulder at Dad, says, "See, it's not so fucking funny when it's *your* mama."

Listen to the children. *Listen to the children!*

So jokes are who I am. If Richard is leaving jokes behind, should I be worried? Will there be no more seeing Richard kill with the jokes I wrote for him? No more gold watches slipped onto my wrist out of gratitude for giving him a great punch line? Most of all, no more feeling the high five from God for making him laugh?

But at Maverick's Flat back in 1969, I don't think about that at all. I'm too busy laughing.

At this point, Richard's making maybe $50,000 a year. (He's blowing about a hundred dollars a day on coke.) He has an album, *Richard Pryor,* out from Reprise that year. He's been on TV, he's appeared in Las Vegas. Richard's been in films—a shitty flop of a film called *The Busy Body,* plus a war movie called *The Green Berets,* with his hero John Wayne, in which his role was left on the cutting-room floor. But at least he has movie credits under his belt.

None of the rest of us at Redd's and Maverick's have been in the movies or on TV or played Vegas or have albums. If you have an album, you aren't supposed to be slumming in

South Central. A record is a ticket out. If you have a comedy album to your credit, you're supposed to be on the Strip or, better yet, onstage in a Las Vegas casino lounge.

But an album doesn't satisfy Richard. Even though the first track of his first album is called "Super Nigger," it's still an album of his Bill Cosby routines. Even "Super Nigger" itself is more or less a Bill Cosby routine, only with a little more edge. Clark Washington, a.k.a. Super Nigger, is a janitor with superpowers. He is "able to see through everything except whitey."

I know if I had an album, a Las Vegas date, or a film role, I'd let myself be happy for at least a little while. Those are the kinds of shots that every stand-up wants to nail. It's what we are all working for. It kills us that Richard has it and it can't make him happy. In fact, it looks like having an album under his belt just makes him even more discontented.

I think about the song "After You Get What You Want, You Don't Want It" from the movie *There's No Business Like Show Business*. "If I gave you the moon, you'd grow tired of it soon."

That is Richard Pryor to a T.

I know from hunting with my granddaddy Preston Ealy that the most dangerous time to be around a snake is right after it sheds its skin. It gets nasty and unpredictable. Richard around this period is jumpy, excitable, and restless. He's climbing the walls in Los Angeles. He's bored with it.

"Mooney, I'm losing my motherfucking mind." It's not the first time he says that to me.

We're parked up the street from Maverick's, at the corner of Martin Luther King Boulevard, only back then it's still just Santa Barbara Avenue.

I'm always up front in the audience at Richard's shows. He likes to hear my laugh. I watch him every night, then he comes offstage and we sit down and go over every little gesture, every word, every nuance. That's what we're doing parked up the street from Maverick's.

Dawn is coming up. The best time in L.A., before all the cars get on the road and the smog hits. Richard drinks from his constant companion, his comforter and security blanket, his bottle of Courvoisier. He pours the brandy into a little paper cup. It fuels a diatribe about his life.

"I'm going crazy," he says again. "This city is driving me nuts."

"So let's leave," I say.

"Yeah, right," he says. "Same old, same old, all over the goddamn country."

"I got to go up home," I say. "Oakland, see Mama, do some clubs. You need to split town for a while, that's where you should go."

"Oakland."

"Oakland, Berkeley, San Francisco."

"Hippies." He laughs. "Them flower chicks don't wear bras, let their titties hang out."

I say, "That bothers you?" He laughs again and shakes his head.

"You know what?" I say. "Whatever Oakland is, it ain't L.A."

He looks over at me, and I can tell that I have him half-convinced. "It ain't L.A.," he repeats softly.

A week later we are rolling up Interstate 5 in my blue Buick. I can see a load lift off Richard's shoulders as Los Angeles slips backward in the rearview mirror. A Motown song, "Ain't Too Proud to Beg," comes on the radio, and we both sing along. "Please don't leave me, girl, don't you go."

Pretty soon we're howling out the lyrics. Then we switch off the radio and Richard starts singing "I Heard It Through the Grapevine" as we pass through Grapevine, California. He's got a quavering voice and can't really hold a note, so I help him along.

Then we go into "My Girl" and "Stop (In the Name of Love)," then practically the whole damn Motown catalog. I'm driving the Buick and Richard's driving his bottle of Courvoisier. I'm getting better mileage than he is.

We start making up fake Motown songs and sing those at the top of our lungs, too. "I gotta girl/My girl's sweet as cream/Every time I see my girl/I let out a scream."

Then we scream our heads off.

Outside in the real world, Richard Nixon runs for president. U.S. Marines kill and get killed in Vietnam. Thurgood Marshall sits as the first black man on the Supreme Court. In Mexico City, sprinters Tommie Smith and John Carlos raise the black-power salute on the medals podium at the Olympics.

All that is happening, but Richard and I are untouchable rolling north on I-5. The dark comes down before the full ugliness of California's Central Valley can hit us. I fall silent. Richard continues tunelessly humming Motown and muttering "Fuck L.A." after nearly every sip of brandy he takes.

He's riding toward a new life.

I'm driving toward an old one.

Mama.

Home.

MAMA
MAMA

CHAPTER 6

"**O**h, hell no!"

Those are my first words. I'm in the womb and I'm screaming out loud, bubbling up the placenta juice, because my world is turning upside down, ass backward, and all-out crazy.

I remember this like it was yesterday. Even if I am a third-trimester fetus at the time.

One minute I am floating safe and warm in my mom's belly. Next second it's like I'm in a blender. Everything's all shook up.

What are you doing, girl, going on a roller coaster when you're sixteen years old and eight months pregnant? I think.

LaVoya Ealy. My mom, my home away from home for the first nine months. Beautiful fresh girlfriend to my dad, George Gladney, basketball star in Shreveport, Louisiana. Just as young as she is.

Carrying me inside her belly, LaVoya's riding on a bus in the shadow of Shreveport's Texas Street Bridge over the Red River. Martin Luther King, Jr.'s birthday, 1941, only MLK is like twelve years old then and nobody knows he's a prophet yet.

The bus driver suddenly gets high or falls asleep or has a stroke or experiences the rapture and drives right off the road. The world turns over and over. Pretty little pregnant teenager banging around like a cue ball on the inside of an upside-down downtown bus.

"Hell, no!" My first words. My first curse against the world. My tiny fist raised in black-power protest, in the womb.

It shakes me up. All I can say is that, looking at the evidence of how my life turns out, I know that *something* did it. Something sets me on a path that isn't like any road anybody else in the world is traveling.

I might as well blame a bus accident that happens before I am born.

My mom's family says that us surviving, me and my mom, is a miracle. They are shocked LaVoya isn't dead, shocked that the unborn-fetus me ain't miscarried all over the highway like some bloody crime scene.

Five weeks later I am birthed out into the world. Against my consent. Still upside down and loopy, a bus-plunge baby, funny as shit and born to shock people.

Shreveport, Louisiana. The deep, deep South. So deep the Confederates there keep right on fighting for weeks after the Civil War ends. Shreveport is where Jefferson Davis is running to when they catch his ass. One of the last die-hard outposts of the Old South.

Back then, Shreveport is what we used to call a "bourgeois" town, meaning a hateful, racist place. Huddie Ledbetter, the great blues singer Lead Belly, hung out a lot in Shreveport.

Lead Belly has a song called "The Bourgeois Blues" that I always think about when I think about Shreveport. Yeah, Lead Belly's song is about Washington, D.C., but he could just as well be singing about Shreveport in the 1940s: "Them white folks . . . they know how/To call a colored man a nigger just to see him bow."

Shreveport is also where the great soul singer Sam Cooke gets arrested in 1963 for making a public disturbance, trying to check into a whites-only Holiday Inn. Cooke pulls up in a $60,000 Maserati, with his band following in a Cadillac limo, and they won't let him in. Racists are such stone-cold imbeciles.

NEGRO BAND LEADER HELD IN SHREVEPORT, reads the *New York Times* headline the next day. The whole incident is Old South all the way.

By 1963, I am long gone from Shreve-town, but fifteen years later I wind up playing Sam Cooke in the movie *The Buddy Holly Story*. By then the story of Sam Cooke's run-in with asshole crackers has taken on the status of legend, and Shreveport has earned its reputation as a racist place.

I leave Louisiana when I am seven years old, but while I'm there I'm not thinking of racism or bourgeois towns or anything like that. I remember my time in Louisiana as though it is surrounded by a golden haze.

A golden haze of family.

A golden haze of Mama.

The key person in my life is my grandmother, my mother's mother, Aimay Ealy, whom everyone inside and outside the family calls Mama. She is the spitting image of the actress Esther Rolle and even embraces some of Esther's no-nonsense characteristics. It's like I am raised by Florida Evans from the TV show *Good Times*. Only I'm not Jimmie Walker.

Mama is the boldest of the bold. No one messes with Mama, and I am her favorite. It is her love during my childhood that shelters me, creates me, molds me into the man I am today. I could never endure the racism and prejudice in Hollywood if not for the strength and character she gives to me.

I am born in a house with a midwife. That's how everyone does it back then. Only women are in the room. The menfolk get kicked out. Everyone is screaming, "Good Lord, here comes Ealy's kid!"

That year, 1941, is the same year a scientist creates plutonium for the first time. Me and plutonium, born simultaneously, both with designs to blow up the world.

Starting at a very young age, too young for me even to remember, I am treated like a very special child. I'm not sure if it is because of my looks, my voice, or my personality, but I am shrouded in some kind of special gold haze, completely protected from racism and prejudice.

My memory of Mama in Shreveport is of an amazing, strong woman. She is really petite but carries herself as though she is ten feet tall. She is so tough, she sleeps with a hammer. Every night, she crawls into bed with a two-pound roofing hammer snugged up against her. Just in case.

Mama raises everyone's kids in town—her own kids, the neighborhood kids, and eventually her grandkids. LaVoya and George are sixteen still, practically babies themselves, so instead of standing by and watching babies raise a baby, Mama takes over. She cares for some white folks in Shreveport, too, cooking, cleaning, sewing, and minding their children.

I have to laugh when I go to downtown Shreveport with Mama. She catches some white kids misbehaving, she whoops their asses and makes them go home. They are scared to death of her. It tickles me. That is one of Mama's supreme lessons. Ain't nobody thinking they're better than us when Mama is in the picture.

Mama wakes up every morning pondering whose ass she is going to whoop. Mama is always whooping ass. My ass, your ass, the neighbor kid's ass. That is her reputation.

"I'm passing out lollipops and whoopin's," she says, "and I'm fresh out of lollipops."

Mama tells me a story from when she's young, and she runs away from home. She has a bandanna tied to a stick with a supply of food inside it.

"I only get as far at the cotton patch," Mama says. "Then I get scared and run back home."

And when she returns, her own mama gives Mama an ass-whooping for running away from home.

Hearing that story makes me laugh the hardest I ever laugh as a kid. I make her tell it to me again and again. The idea of Mama, the ultimate ass-whooper, getting a whoopin' herself, makes me laugh until my gut hurts.

I think this is what makes me a comic. The world going upside down and butt backward plants the seed of all my comedy, still to this day. Mama giving an ass-whoopin' ain't funny, because it's expected. Mama *getting* an ass-whoopin', now that's hilarious. I learn early on that flipping the world butt backward and saying the unexpected in the punch line is funny.

Mama's husband is Preston Ealy, a Jamaican with Caddo and European blood in him. I call him Daddy. He looks like Jane Fonda's daddy, Henry. Daddy Preston is a hunter. He goes out after small game nearly every day, bringing back food for the family stew pot.

Daddy: Preston Ealy, my grandfather and a great outdoorsman

Later on in my life, when Richard Pryor is going crazy shooting up his own house, I am able to go up there and deal with him and all his guns because of my experiences as a child hunting with Daddy Preston. He gives me my good grounding in weaponry. It comes in handy.

My Shreveport life is all Mama and Daddy and uncles and aunts and cousins. And the Church. Daddy Preston's brother, my uncle Shank, is a minister. His other brother, Uncle Tip, is a deacon and an outrageous drunk.

Mama's best friend in Shreveport is this witch lady, Miss Amerae. She is Creole and looks Indian. She makes her own potions and poultices. Miss Amerae practices voodoo and can predict the future.

Miss Amerae is like the boogie-woman of my childhood. She scares the pants off me. She chews tobacco and spits it out in big spouts of brown phlegm. She speaks in broken French.

"I can make a snake kiss a chicken and a cat kiss a dog!" she says. She tells us her five husbands all get sick and die after eating mushrooms. Her sixth husband won't eat mushrooms, so he conveniently "falls" off a cliff.

Miss Amerae has no children, but she does have a pet goat named Willie. I wake up with nightmares when I'm five years old, thinking about Willie's Satan eyes. Whenever Mama sends me over to her house to borrow baking soda or snuff or pig's feet or whatever, I face off with Willie. He looks at me like he's going to take my soul.

I slip past Willie, go inside, and politely say, "Hi, Miss Amerae." I never look at her. I stare at the floor. Miss Amerae gives me what Mama wants. I say, "Bye, Miss Amerae." I don't want to make that woman mad at me.

When we misbehave, Mama says she's going to get Miss Amerae to put a spell on us if we don't act right. Women around town go to Miss Amerae for abortions. I hear everyone talking about it. White folks, black folks, Indians, they all go to Miss Amerae to get fixed. She knows where all the bodies are buried. A few of them are buried in her own backyard.

Mama has a lot of African ways. When she is cold or in pain, she hums. We all love us some humming. Mama hums to heal. I'm humming right now just thinking about it . . . *Hummmmmmmmmmmm, ah-hummmmmmm.*

Later on in life, when I encounter mantras and meditation and all that New Age business, I hear people chanting the holy Hindu syllable *Om* and I recognize it right away. It's Mama's hum.

The Sanctifying Church we go to is the American one that's the most like African religion. I get sanctified myself when I am five. The parishioners lift me up, pass me around, and then carry me out, like kids at a rave.

Folks speak in tongues. The better the actor you are, the more popular you are in church. Aunt Katie can act. She is always feeling the spirit. Mama accuses her of doing it just to show her ass. My aunt Erma Lee always wants to preach. But the town is sexist. They won't allow women to be preachers. They look on her like she is a demon.

The same people come to church every week, screaming "Help me, Jesus!" and "Lord have mercy!" People have fits and ask for a healing when they're sick with gout or arthritis. They are always jumping around trying to cast out the devil.

Years later, when I happen to encounter a man on the Santa Monica Promenade having an epileptic seizure, I think he is rolling around, talking in tongues. I walk by him and say, "Amen!" It's my Pentecostal upbringing.

People confess their sins to my uncle Shank, the minister. One parishioner confesses to sleeping with another man's wife. It turns out it is Uncle Shank's wife. Uncle Shank starts wailing on him, and the two have a fistfight right there in church.

The church teaches us lessons about how things are between black folks and white folks. We are always going out in groups from our congregation. I see how careful everyone is in public, putting on a different face for the white people to see.

At a church picnic, Mama tells me that the word *picnic* comes from white people lynching black people. *Picnic* is short for *pick a nig*.

"They pick a nigger, any nigger they want," she says, "lynch him, and then have a family picnic."

Anyone still hungry after that? I know now that it's not true, that it ain't where the word comes from, but as a child the idea makes a deep impression on me.

Early on, I become convinced that my aunt Katie Gates's son has formed a poisonous jealousy of me. I'm the cute one. I got the face people go to the plastic surgeon to get.

As a child, I always think Bobby Gates is ugly as sin. He's so homely and ill-favored, you have to tie a pork chop to that boy just to get a dog to play with him. So naturally Bobby despises me. It is my first experience of something that happens to me all through my life: being hated on because I'm good-looking.

So when Bobby fools around with fire and burns our house down, I'm certain it's me he's after. Nobody else is at home.

I'm five years old. I see smoke curling up in the hallway outside the room. I know the house in on fire. So what do I do? With the scared-ass logic of a five-year-old, I hide under the bed. I imagine Bobby, watching pretty Paul burn up, rubbing his hands together and laughing like a movie villain.

Only I didn't burn. My aunt Pressie comes wailing into the house, drags me out from under the bed, and runs out of the house with me in her arms. She's screaming and flailing and I'm snuggling in her embrace as quiet as the baby Jesus.

Outside the house is a big crowd of family, all crying and worrying over whether I'm okay. It's like a warm bath of love. Bobby's fire backfires and I survive. I'm just doted on all the more.

Everyone in Shreveport loves them some Ealys, except maybe Bobby and one other creature. It's our neighbor's parrot, Feathers. Feathers screams out "Nigger" all day long, every single day. It's the only fucking word he knows. Everyone in the neighborhood can hear it.

Maybe it's only fitting. The first time I hear the word *nigger*, it's out of the mouth of a parrot. All my life, I hear that word parroted mindlessly, and I think of Feathers.

Mama hates on that parrot. Really hates the bird. No one ever calls her "nigger." Not to her face. Nobody even thinks it. They are either too scared, too much in awe, or too loving. Them white folks she works for, they take care of her like she is pure gold.

We stay in Louisiana until I am seven. A whole lotta black folks move North at the end of the 1940s to find better jobs. We are among them. No discussion. Mama just announces it.

"Let's pack our bags," she says. "We're moving to Oakland."

I'm wondering, *Oakland? Where's that?*

Oak Land. That's how I pronounce it. Like it's two words.

Mama sends Daddy on ahead. He rents us a house. So we get on the train, all our belongings packed with us, and embark on our new life.

As soon as we leave the station, Mama leans over to me. "Well, we're never gonna have to hear that parrot say 'nigger' no more. You know why?"

"'Cause we're going to Oak Land, Mama?"

"Nope," she says, grinning. "Because I poisoned it!"

We laugh at that as we leave Louisiana behind. Looking out the train windows is like watching a movie for me. I sit on Mama's lap and watch the countryside roll past.

I have a fantasy as a child about what would happen if the black people take over and run things. Mostly it involves me having all the candy I want, a bigger house, a nicer car, Mama retired at her ease, and Daddy wearing a nice suit.

But as that train travels through East Texas and then hits

the plains, I think, *This country is too big for black people to run*. The train goes a little farther, and now we're in the grasslands that never end. I think, *This country is too big for white people to run, too.*

Why don't we just run it together? Nice fantasy, child. I fall asleep to the clickety-clack of the train wheels.

CHAPTER 7

I never much realize I am a Negro until we move to Oakland. My Shreveport life is such a warm cocoon that even if we are in the racist South, I don't see myself as anything but loved. The whole Ealy clan, friends and family both, eventually relocates to California.

In Oakland, Daddy Preston rents the family a two-story house on 18th Street, in the middle of the ghetto. But the Oakland ghetto back then isn't all black. Our neighbors on one side are Portuguese, and Mexican on the other. Across the street from our house is Gilmore Steel, owned by a Jewish family.

Italians, Jews, Irish, all cram in side by side. It's not all black, but it is all poor. It's the first time I hear the word *nigger* used both ways—as a slur and as a term of affection. Mama can kill the parrot, but she can't stop all the people in the Oakland ghetto who toss around that word as if it's nothing.

■ ■ ■

On the first floor of our house is a storefront, and to bring in cash, Mama opens up a little convenience store, selling eggs, bread, milk, and the kind of small, everyday sundries that people in the neighborhood forever need. She sells cold Coca-Cola in ten-ounce bottles for five cents.

It's odd, but though we are in the middle of the most built-up part of Oakland, it's as though I have a rural childhood. For pets, I raise the wild animals that Daddy Preston captures and brings home. I keep a whole menagerie: a red fox, a bantam-tailed rooster, a rabbit, and a chicken that I call Turkey. Daddy brings me a baby raccoon that I name Sam. Turkey chases Sam until he grows up and gets a little bigger. From then on, Sam chases Turkey. Turnabout is fair play.

Even living in the ghetto, Daddy Preston still manages to hunt. He goes up into the Oakland hills and shoots possum, raccoons, rabbits, and snakes, and drives farther up into the mountains after black bear.

Mama stews up everything he kills. I eat it all. My favorite dish is beef neck bones and butter beans. You can take the family out of the South, but you can't take the South out of the family.

Mama can cook her ass off. She knows her way around a kitchen. She grows her own herbs and has a vegetable garden in the backyard. She makes her own butter. Everything in her house is fresh.

It's on 18th Street that Mama first calls me Mooney. She never says why. Maybe I am a sloe-eyed, moony child, dreamy-looking. Mama starts calling me Mooney, and then suddenly everyone else is calling me that, too. Pretty soon that's how I think of myself. I am not Paul Ealy or Paul Gadney. I am Paul Mooney.

Nicknames are a thing with us. Everyone has one. We all have celebrity look-alikes, too. My mother LaVoya's nickname is Didaree. She has the makings of Dorothy Dandridge and Diahann Carroll. Her older sister Katherine, my aunt Katie, looks like Tina Turner. My mother's baby sister Pressie is a dead ringer for Eartha Kitt. She's a hoofer, a tap dancer, and I get my dancing skills from her. My mother's brother, my uncle Buddy, looks just like Sidney Poitier. There are also my other uncles, Tip and Shank.

Nicknames and look-alikes are running jokes. They create the world of my childhood. "Look at Sidney Poitier, running off to the john!" somebody calls out, as Uncle Buddy hotfoots it to the bathroom. Everyone cracks up. I get a lot of my comedy from the Ealy family.

All the time I am in Oakland, I can feel change coming. I am at DeFremery Park, just down the street from our house, and there's some sort of political rally there. This handsome white man is grabbing everybody by the hand, and he's got the mayor of San Francisco with him. He's somebody. He looks like a movie star and he carries himself as though he thinks everybody else should know that he's somebody. He's got better hair than Elvis.

It's the first time I see a white man that black people love so much. I hear other people in the crowd say over and over, he is going to be president. I don't believe them. The white man is too young. Presidents are old, saggy-faced white men, like Eisenhower. Then I hear Mama say it, too. "That man is going to be president some day."

So when he comes around to me, I move up front in the crowd and reach out. I say, "You are going to be president." JFK flashes that big toothy Boston Irish grin at me and shakes my hand.

In Oakland, I see LaVoya, my real mother, more than I

ever did in Shreveport. My father George Gladney stayed in Shreveport and faded out of my life, but my mother is always in and out of the Oakland house with my aunt Katie. The two women are fast. Aunt Pressie can't keep up with them. At one time, they are both playing softball on an all-girl's team and are members of a motorcycle club.

Later days: My mother, LaVoya Ealy, and me in front of my cherry red Caddy

I only slowly wake up to what is going on with Mother and Aunt Katie. They are riding back and forth to L.A. on motorcycles. They bring back furs, designer clothes, jewelry. I think, well, we're rich. Then I realize that my aunt and mother know all the boosters in the neighborhood.

"Can I get a quarter?" I ask my mother one afternoon.

She looks at me as though she is about to cry. "Oh, honey," she says, "I don't have a quarter—I don't even have a dime."

She does burst into tears then, and brings me into her arms and hugs me. "I'm sorry," she says over and over.

I realize just how poor we are. Money comes in waves, but sometimes the tide stays out a long time. We get flush once when I am thirteen, when LaVoya works at a jazz club. At first she's a cleaning lady, but there's a push on to integrate jobs. The management suddenly realizes how pretty my mama is, and they make her a waitress.

When she comes in at three or four in the morning, I help her count her tips. The dollar bills smell like beer. Even though my mother lives a very risqué lifestyle, she never lets a man stay overnight at our house.

My mother's always sorry about something, but not sorry enough to stop taking money from her son. I'm working in the cucumber fields that summer, and I get a few bills and some coins for pay—and all the cucumbers I can lug home.

Mom waits for me. "Darling," she says as soon as I come in the door, hot and sweaty from working in the fields. "Where's your money? Give it here quick!"

I am naive. I see all the men in my family giving money to their girlfriends. Since I am always giving my mom money, I figure she is my girlfriend.

Mama catches wind of this and wises me up. We decide to keep all of my money in Mama's bra, since that's her equivalent of hiding it under the mattress. There's a lot of room in there. My money goes into the left cup. I always know where it is. I do my business at the Bank of Mama's Left Tit.

Mama doesn't trust banks. She never goes to a bank except to add money to our Christmas fund. Even if it is only two dollars, she puts money in every week so we have something under the tree.

Under Mama's stern influence, my mother slowly turns her life around. She's approaching thirty, and she can't go around with bikers and ballplayers forever. She goes back to school to get her nursing degree. She does real estate. LaVoya loses her wild ways and becomes a respected person in the community.

All along I cling to Mama, my rock.

Mama has the greatest expressions. "A dog that will bring a bone will take a bone." Meaning don't trust anyone who's too subservient. "A new broom knows how to sweep the floor, but an old broom knows where the dirt is." "The grass is always greener on the other side of the fence, but don't forget what they have to put on that grass to keep it green." "Birds fly high, but they have to come to the ground to get water."

When scammers come around the house trying to borrow money, Mama tells everyone, "A cow always knows where the weak fence is." She never wants people to take advantage of us or treat us badly.

Some of her phrases are adults-only, directed toward the women of the family. "A hard dick knows no names." "Never buy a man shoes—he'll walk away from you." My favorite is what she says to the women when they come home after staying out all night or being gone a few days.

"You dumb bitches!" she yells at them. "I don't fatten frogs to feed snakes. Are you stupid? I taught you better than that. A wet pussy and a dry purse don't match."

Solid wisdom.

My own introduction to sex comes soon after we move to Oakland. My two best friends are some Portuguese kids from the neighborhood, a brother and sister. We go to Cole Elementary School, a few blocks away from my house, on 10th Street. Every morning the sister screams from outside my bedroom window. She yells, "Wake up, Mooney, wake up!"

I come to the window and scream out, "I'll be right down!" Because I don't wear pajamas but sleep in my birthday suit, I always show up at the window naked as a jaybird. This might be what gives her ideas. One afternoon in my bedroom, when Mama and Daddy aren't at home, she rapes me.

There is nothing else to call it. I am eight, she is twelve years old. She has a movie magazine. She opens it to show me the pictures. We start out by imitating the kissing she sees in one photograph.

She rubs herself all over me. I don't know what is happening, but it feels good. She pulls her shirt down and her skirt up, jumps on top of me, and wriggles and bucks until I come.

Unlike other people who are raped, I like it. Because she and I have sex, I believe that I am automatically in love. I want so badly to marry her. I go to her parents and ask solemnly for their approval.

Her mom and dad say no. Of course, I think it is because I am black. Or the fact that I am eight years old. To my surprise, they say no because I am not Catholic.

For her sake (and for the sake of the feeling I get when she rubs up against me), I try to become Catholic. I study the catechism. I get stickers of the saints. But marrying her becomes a problem. The one day I go to Mass, I have sore knees. I conclude that I can't become a Catholic because I can't kneel in church.

Her brother is still my best friend. The Christmas before I turn ten, Mama uses her bank money to buy me a Lone Ranger and Tonto costume set.

"Let's play," I say to him. "I want to be the Lone Ranger."

He says, "No, I'm white and you're not. You look more like the Indian. You be Tonto."

Right about then is when I start to hate him.

CHAPTER 8

When I am fourteen years old, my mother moves us out of Oakland, north across the freeway to Berkeley. She's trying to straighten out her life and get away from the crowd she runs with.

This is the first time in my young life that I am away from the constant loving atmosphere that surrounds Mama. Even though she and Daddy live only ten miles away, I feel as though I have been shoved out of the nest.

So what do I do? I try desperately to find that same level of love elsewhere—and that's when I discover a truth that changes my life. I find out that applause equals love.

I become the hambone king of Berkeley, California. It's a popular song and a dance craze at the time.

That year, 1955, a lot of bands, both white and black, come out with versions of the hambone song, which is basically an old minstrel tune with a lot of different variations. "Hambone, hambone, have you heard? Papa's gonna buy me a mockingbird."

More than anything, hambone is a beat, done with palms hitting your chest or leg: *slap-lacka-lacka-slap-slap*. The Milwaukee drummer Red Saunders and his orchestra have a hit with his version, the whiter-than-white Bell Sisters, too, and the country singer Tennessee Ernie Ford. Everybody is doing it. Later on, Bo Diddley takes it over and makes it rock and roll. Johnny Otis's rock hit "Willie and the Hand Jive" is just another version of the song.

All the local movie theaters have hambone dance contests before the shows. Grand prize, ten dollars, sometimes fifteen or twenty-five.

My best friends, Brother and Sammy, get me up onstage for the first time at the Oakland Paramount when we get to the theater early for the matinee one Saturday afternoon. I still recall the feature: *Mister Roberts* with Henry Fonda.

"Sign up, kids!" announces the movie emcee. "Dance for the prize!"

"Come on, Mooney," Sammy says. "I seen you do it. You can win!"

I know I can hambone with the best of them. You pop your fingers and twist out your knees. I hear that beat in the cradle. I've been doing hambone for Mama since I learn how to walk. Nobody's got anything on me.

So I get up onstage at the Oakland Paramount and win the whole contest.

I don't realize it back then, but the hambone is juba, a slave rhythm brought from West Africa. The reason they slap their bodies is that the masters don't allow them to have drums. Too dangerous. The darkies might be passing messages to one another. They might be plotting to kill us in our sleep. No drums allowed.

There are just a few hundred kids in the Paramount audience that afternoon, and a lot of popcorn flying around, and not everybody is paying attention, but I'm bitten by the performance bug, and bitten good.

Applause is love. I'm up there, and I know it. I feel that the audience is loving me, they are with me all the way, with Sammy laughing and the faces of the girls in the front row shining up at me.

Slap-lacka-lacka-slap-slap.

It all starts at that moment.

I like the way the sawbuck feels in my hand when the emcee slips me the first-prize money afterward. I like the way people look at me when I come off the stage. I like Brother and Sammy pounding me on the back, celebrating my triumph.

I like it all. I want to do it again and again. But the lights in the theater go down, the movie starts, and Henry Fonda comes on the screen. To this day, I hate that movie, *Mister Roberts.*

We all go to Luther Burbank Junior High in Berkeley. Sammy, Brother, and I laugh about Luther Burbank's last words: "I don't feel good." We are always saying that to one another and then fake dying. Even though the students are mostly white, the school has a few black teachers, so I feel comfortable there.

The Monday after I win the hambone contest, I can tell my popularity in school has skyrocketed. Students, especially girls, talk about me in the halls. I see my path in life. I will be the Hambone King. Brother and Sammy act as my managers. They scout around for movie theaters holding hambone contests. We go to the Orinda, the Shattuck, the California, and the Oaks. Sometimes Sammy and Brother come up onstage and back me up. We have a routine.

I always win, time after time. Brother, Sammy, and I get real excited. We're going to make thousands of dollars by taking our act out on the road. We plot our moves in my bedroom at the 18th Street house in Oakland. We're going to run away from home. We think we're doing our secret planning on the downlow, but of course, Mama knows all, sees all.

"Circus broke down, did you hear?" she says casually, as we come downstairs to the kitchen to raid the fridge.

"Yeah?" I say, cautious. Something's up, I can tell from Mama's tone.

"Black panther escaped," she says.

"A panther?" Sammy says. His eyes go wide.

"You know why they call 'em black panthers, don't you?" Mama says. "Them cats just loves to eat young black children."

Brother and Sammy stare at her. I laugh nervously. "Mama, you're joking us!"

"Yum," Mama says, smacking her lips. "Tasty black kids."

By unspoken agreement, Brother, Sammy, and I immediately abandon our plans to leave home. We decide it's better to stay right where we are.

It turns out I don't have to go anywhere. Fame, celebrity, and show business come to hunt me down where I live.

CHAPTER 9

It's 1955, the height of the boring, bland, and white Eisenhower years. Marian Anderson is the first black singer to perform at the Metropolitan Opera. Fourteen-year-old Emmett Till is murdered in Money, Mississippi, for allegedly whistling at a white woman, Carolyn Bryan. Rosa Parks is arrested in Montgomery, and Dr. Martin Luther King, Jr., organizes a boycott of city buses.

Racism is a terrible weight to live with. What an awful trip to lay on anyone, but especially on a young child. Whoever dismisses bigotry or underestimates its impact has never lived under the pain. During those years, first at Luther Burbank and later at Berkeley High School, I'm immune in a personal sense. I see examples of racism plenty of times, like slights in class, with teachers ignoring black students to call on their pet white kids. But I myself feel too secure to be touched by anything like that. It just offends my sense of justice.

My anger boils just beneath the surface. I think about someone telling a small kid he's second-class because he's

Berkeley High School:
My yearbook photo

black. He's just an innocent child, and someone sticks a knife into his soul. It's repellent, and those responsible, and those who stand by and watch it happen, will burn in hell.

All around me, my friends and acquaintances buckle under the burden of bigotry and prejudice and ignorance. I can look in their eyes and witness it happening. They get haunted. Their eyes tell me what's going on in their hearts. *Well, maybe I am a low piece of shit like they say I am.*

That never happens to me. Maybe it's just the luck of personality or the buffer that Mama's love gives me. It's water off my back. But at my junior high school graduation ceremony, I duck out from under my black face for the first time ever.

As usual, a girl is involved. I'm going out with a white girl named Judy. I only talk to her on the phone and at school. Her parents don't know I am black, because when I call the house, I put on a great white voice.

For graduation, the dress code requires us to wear a black or navy suit. But the rules never apply to me. I insist that my mother buy me a beige suit because I want to stand out.

Even back then, I love fashion. I am fly! Everyone in school knows that I am going to be the only one to wear a light-colored suit. Judy calls me up the night before our graduation, crying. She is scared that her parents will find out that I am black. And since I will be the only one in beige, I know I'll stand out.

I love Judy so much that when they announce my name to come up and get my diploma, I hide backstage. I never show my face, so her parents won't see me and find out who I am.

Mama and my mother are furious at me. They don't know my motives. I think it will make them even more angry if they know what game I am playing. It isn't until years later that I finally tell them the truth. They had forgotten all about the incident by then, but it sears itself into my memory.

My skulking around backstage doesn't seem like cowardice to me. I think I am doing it for love.

Other indignities, large and small, assault me at Berkeley High. Every black person in the world has that watershed "nigger" moment, a time when they remember being called the *N* word. It's burned deep into our brains. It can never be washed out.

In high school with me are twin white girls, and one of them gives me my very own personal nigger moment. I guess they aren't identical twins, because her sister is very liberal, but she is racist to the bone. We are in typing class (yes, I type), and when the teacher leaves the room one time, I get up to walk around.

I accidentally kick over the racist twin's bag, and ever the

Mama-trained gentleman, I am going to pick it up and apologize, when this white girl says, "Pick it up!" Like a command.

"What did you say?" I ask her. She looks at me with hate. Her sister puts an arm around her, but Bigot Twin shakes it off.

"Pick up your own goddamn purse," I say.

"Pick up my purse, nigger!" She slaps my face, hard.

The Lord channels me. I grab her blond stringy hair and drag her toward the window.

Her twin is screaming. Everyone in class is shouting at me.

"Don't throw her out the window, Mooney! Don't throw her out!"

The teacher comes back in to see me grabbing a handful of Bigot Twin's hair. Then it's the principal's office, followed by the police station. I am too proud to tell anyone but Mama what triggered me.

Racism is worked into the whole institution of Berkeley High back then. The school officials don't allow me to work at the yearbook or school newspaper. Again, I don't mope over the mistreatment. I just go ahead and publish my own guerilla newspaper. It's a smash hit. I get called to the principal's office, where the assistant principal says they will suspend me if I continue to publish.

"This is not allowed," the assistant principal says. He's a guy whose ugly black horn-rims cover half his face. It is against school policy, he explains, for a student to bootleg a newspaper.

School policy. Yeah, that must be a clause in the rules that they invent just for me, because there ain't anyone else around who is running a guerrilla publishing operation.

It doesn't matter to me, and Mr. Horn Rims can tell it doesn't matter, and that makes him all the more uptight and angry. Mooney must be heeled like a dog. Mooney must be chastened.

But I'm not chastened. Far from it. I am sixteen years old, tall, skinny, and good-looking. Nothing bothers me. On the first day that I legally can, I go down and pass my driver's test. My mother's fast lifestyle is good for something. She owns a beautiful canary yellow Ford convertible. Me sitting behind the wheel of that car turns out to be irresistible.

Maybe a little too irresistible. A girl named Toni can't resist me, and I can't resist her, either. We have sex in the back of the Ford convertible, parked up in the Oakland hills under the night stars.

Once again, sex equals marriage in my young mind. I immediately conclude I am going to walk down the aisle with Toni. All the boys talk about whom they are going to marry and I always say it will be Toni. She and I are going to be together forever.

Only it doesn't work out that way. Instead, after a few months, Toni mysteriously disappears from view. She won't return my calls, either. I am frantic. I can't understand what is happening. Then I hear through the grapevine that Toni is pregnant.

I am young and terrified. Mama is furious with me, and my mother, too. I never know when Toni gives birth because her family keeps it from me. When I do find out, I am in school and almost die. And then I hear that she has given birth to twins. I collapse, literally, right there in the halls of Berkeley High School.

When I show up at the 18th Street house, Mama makes fun of me by doing a singsong ghetto rhyme.

Annie has a baby in the back of a Caddy
Annie say the baby don't look like daddy
Annie give her baby a pat on the head
Baby say to Annie my daddy ain't Ted
Annie has a baby she can't go to school
Annie say the daddy is a stone-cold fool

She laughs and laughs, and I steam. The situation isn't much funny to me. Twins! I'm the father of two baby boys! Daryl and Duane Mooney. As the twins grow up, I do see them, but I'm not a big part of their lives, because Toni's great-grandmother keeps them from me. It's not until much later, when I move to L.A., that I start to see them regularly.

Toward the end of high school, I fall in with half dozen beautiful women, all in their late teens and all beauty-contest winners. My cousin Alice is one of them, and the Global sisters: Joanne, Sally, and Cynthia. Diane DeMarko is among them, too. She has just won the Miss Albany contest, in a town immediately north of Berkeley. Now she and Alice are up for Miss Oakland.

I am in heaven with these women. Even though none of us are fucking each other, the aura of sex and beauty and youth is intoxicating. Diane has wealthy parents, and we tool around in her little two-seater Mercedes sports car. I take the whole group on forays of what I call "nig-noggin'"—slang for going to black dance halls like the Clef, Bop City, the Long Bar, or the Orbit Room.

The only other male we allow into our group is Huey P. Newton. He's a long way from being the Black Panther he's going to become. He and I get along well because he's another Louisiana boy whose family uproots and moves to Oakland. I know him some in Oakland, but when I move to Berkeley, Huey shows up at Berkeley High, too.

I think Huey transfers schools because he likes me, but he's really more interested in my cousin Alice. Alice at age seventeen is one of the most beautiful women I have ever seen or ever will see. Light, light skin and startling green eyes. The way she carries herself, with a quiet grace, makes her prettiness all the more pronounced.

Huey loves Alice. He wants to marry her. Back then, even though he goes through school, he can't read. He's starting his self-education. He carries a copy of Plato's *Republic* around everywhere he goes. The dude is struggling, moving his lips as he tries to get through one of the most difficult books of all time.

Our aim in founding the State was not the dispropor-tionate happiness of any one class, but the greatest hap-piness of the whole; we thought that in a State which is ordered with a view to the good of the whole we should be most likely to find Justice, and in the ill-ordered State injustice: and, having found them, we might then decide which of the two is the happier.

Whew! That's some dense shit right there. I think about poor Huey, puzzling his way through it. It's all Greek to me. But he doesn't give up. He masters it and goes on to become one of the founders of the Black Panthers.

Back then, though, he is just Huey, the only guy on the block who can compete with me in being handsome. All the girls love them some Huey P. Newton. Alice just accepts his worship and doesn't go any further with him. I wonder how the course of African-American politics might have changed if my gorgeous cousin Alice would have looked kindly upon Huey's love pleas.

It ain't Huey's time yet, not with Alice, not with Plato,

not with the Panthers. It's still the 1950s. The country is in an Eisenhower-Nixon coma. Ideas about race and culture are frozen solid, as though they're encased in a block of ice.

Me just being me helps them unfreeze a little.

In 1959, the biggest thing to hit Bay Area television is Dick Stewart's *Dance Party* program, broadcast every day except Sunday on KPIX Channel 5, a CBS affiliate. *Dance Party*'s afternoon time slot goes from low ratings to crazily popular almost overnight.

Dick Stewart is the squareball of all squareballs, a Hollywood big-band crooner who comes back to his hometown of Oakland to host the show. He plays a Jimmy Dorsey song as the theme music for a dance program aimed at teenagers! He's plastic and tan-fastic, with a big fake showbiz smile, but I like him.

Dance Party features a group of teenagers called "regulars," who appear on every show and dance to the Top 40 tunes of the day. It's the West Coast answer to Philly's *American Bandstand*. Both shows are hosted by guys named Dick. *Bandstand* goes national a couple years before on ABC.

Tickets to be in the studio for the live *Dance Party* broadcast are hard to get, and getting to be a regular is nearly impossible. Naturally, that's what I set my sights on.

On a Monday morning I skip school and head across the bridge to the KPIX studios on Van Ness in San Francisco. I figure I'll show up during off hours when the live program isn't being broadcast, since the staff won't be so busy then. My strategy works. I walk right into the office and ask a secretary to introduce me to the producer of *Dance Party*.

It turns out he's standing right there, a tall, light-haired guy named Dave Parker. "I'd like to dance on the show," I say.

"We have auditions for that," Parker says. But I can tell by the way he's looking me up and down that he's interested.

"I've won about a half dozen dance contests," I say hurriedly. I run through my resume—the Paramount, the Orinda, every area theater that has a hambone competition.

"You can dance?" he says.

"Oh, I can dance," I say.

Parker looks at the secretary for a woman's point of view. She gives him a slight nod.

"Okay," he says. "You're in, but you're on probation."

It isn't the last time that my good looks help me skip the grueling, emotionally draining audition process.

"When do I start?"

Parker looks at his wristwatch. "The show goes on in six hours," he says.

"Today?"

"I'll see you at three o'clock," he says, and shakes my hand before disappearing into the interior of the studio.

My girlfriends are all crazy excited, especially Diane De-Marko, who is a dancer, but they're full of advice for me at the same time. They all want to tell me what to wear, but I know already. I choose a light yellow shirt and a pair of beige linen pants with cream-colored bucks for my outfit. I am stylin'!

The *Dance Party* set is a cheap plywood mock-up of a soda fountain. The room is a lot smaller than it looks on TV. I show up, the new dancer, amid a couple dozen regulars who all know one another. Most of them are white, but there are black girls and Asian girls, too.

They freak when they see me. Racially freak. They've never seen anything like me. The white kids on *Dance Party* are white as snow. They could drop dead from being white.

They are critically white. It sounds like a cliché, but I find out that they cannot keep a beat.

They can be choreographed, but they can't feel the rhythm the way I can. They hop around like rabbits, doing the dances of the day. The Swim, the Twist, the Mashed Potato, and the Monster Mash. Then the whole dance menagerie: the Monkey, the Chicken, the Roach, the Pony.

Dance Party plays up the romances between the regulars. It's like a variety show with a little bit of soap opera thrown in. Dick Stewart sets the stage for romantic "silhouette" dances, with designated couples slow dancing beneath a mirrored ball. The audience avidly follows the ups and downs of the teenage romances, and the regulars are all local celebrities.

The hot couple of the day is Lynn Facciola and Frank Pisa. They get fan mail and field autograph requests whenever they go out in public. They are *Dance Party*'s version of *American Bandstand*'s superpopular couple, Bob Clayton and Justine Carelli.

But the star of the show is a European-born beauty named Barbara Goutscher. Even though she barely resembles movie star Sandra Dee, she wins a Gidget lookalike contest to get her place on the show (she also wins a date with *Gidget*'s leading man, James Darren).

Later on, Barbara goes Hollywood and changes her last name to Bouchet. She has a long career in TV and plays Miss Moneypenny in the 1967 satirical Bond film, *Casino Royale*. I freak out when I happen across an episode of *Star Trek* and see my old *Dance Party* regular Barbara playing Kelinda, the Kelvan seductress, and making out with Captain Kirk!

A handful of the regulars come out of *Dance Party* to go on to Hollywood careers. Barbara Burrus changes her name to Anne Randall and becomes *Playboy* magazine's May 1967

Playmate. She eventually winds up marrying the *Dance Party* host, Dick Stewart.

The whole vibe on set is one of raging teenage hormones. I crack up laughing because Dick Stewart has a habit of staring at the tits of the female regulars who are big chested.

One regular, Archie, falls head over heels for Aasa, a blond ice-queen type. The problem is, Archie is darker skinned, with some Native-American blood in him. He winds up facing off with Aasa's father on her front lawn, the girl trying to hold her dad back from pummeling her forbidden teenage love.

In this atmosphere, what am I going to do? If I have to dance only with the same two regular girls who are black, it's going to cut my possibilities way down. I don't even think about it. Every day I am running with a whole flock of white women, integrated by me and my cousin Alice. Why should *Dance Party* be any different?

I dance with the black girls, the Asian girls, the white girls. I dance with everyone. It's natural. It's not a thought-out move on my part. But in my own way, I'm integrating American television. I get my beautiful cousin Alice on the show. She dances with all the white boys.

Dance Party gets hate mail. "I don't want some big nigger dancing with white girls!" Vile stuff. I have to credit Dave Parker and Dick Stewart, though. They never backtrack. They can't. I'm unstoppable. I am too popular.

American Bandstand, on the other side of the country, practices strict racial separation. It fights against integration fiercely and to the end, like a lady wrestler. That's the whole subject of John Waters's *Hairspray,* the hit movie and Broadway musical.

I meet lots of celebrities on *Dance Party.* All the big stars appear on the show. Ann-Margret. James Brown. Annette

Funicello. Clint Eastwood. Aretha. The Big Bopper and Ritchie Valens, just days before the plane crash that becomes the day the music died.

"Are you coming back on the show?" I ask Ann-Margret as she sweeps out of the *Dance Party* studio on a cloud of perfume.

"I don't know," she says, giving me her flirtiest smile. "Are you going to be here?"

The one day in my life I wish I could do over is when Sam Cooke comes to the *Dance Party* studio. That afternoon I am off in Stockton picking peaches. So I never meet the greatest soul singer in the world, and the man who I will play in a movie.

Applause is love, and so is the TV camera. I'm a *Dance Party* regular, and I feel as though I am the king of California. I get recognized and asked for autographs out on the street.

The closing theme of *Dance Party*, played at the end of every show, is "Dream" by the Pied Pipers—one of Dick Stewart's schmaltzy big-band throwbacks. "Dream when the day is through/Dream then they might come true."

I am living a dream that I didn't even know I had. The thing about dreams, though, is that when you realize one, it just whets your appetite for an even bigger dream. At the dawn of a new decade, in a lesbian bar in the beatnik area of North Beach, I discover someone who sets me on a whole new path.

CHAPTER 10

In my last year of high school, I date a pretty girl named Karen Perry. She looks like a combination of actresses Lori Petty and Audrey Hepburn. Karen and my cousin Alice are best friends. People always think that they're sisters. Karen is a great actress herself, and plays the female lead in all the school productions at Berkeley High.

The school has a double standard for its plays. The drama teachers want only white kids to perform. I audition and get rejected.

"Paul, we just don't have a part for you." A polite rejection, but I see right through it. I don't have the complexion for the protection. White people like to think their skin color protects them. I don't have it, so they can ignore me. I'm dancing on the top-rated teen TV show, and you don't have a part for me?

But I always have to be onstage. I always have to guerrilla my shit. In direct opposition to the drama teachers, I start my own talent show. I do a skit based on *Little Red Riding Hood,* and I play the wolf, of course. I look out at the school audience, and whoever isn't laughing their guts out is shifting uncomfortably in their chairs.

That's how I like it. You either laugh, or you get uptight.

I have sex with Karen, the drama department's major star, and she gets pregnant. No more school plays for her. She gives birth to our daughter, Lisa. I am not out of high school yet, and I have three children.

As the 1960s dawn, I'm getting more and more restless. *Dance Party* is great and my first taste of celebrity is sweet, but suddenly Oakland, Berkeley, San Francisco—the whole place seems too small to hold me. I look around for options. I attend a local community college, but that seems more small-time than ever.

The *Dance Party* gig ends abruptly when I get drafted into the army and sent to West Germany. I think maybe that will satisfy my thirst for the wider world, but I learn quickly that there's nothing more claustrophobic than the U.S. Army. I had sergeants constantly on my jock.

My main army claim to fame is integrating the base swimming pools. They make me a lifeguard. The little kids who come to the pools look up at me, sitting all regal on my lifeguard's throne, and they give me shit.

"That nigger's the boss?" one kid says.

My sergeant is there. "Anybody calls my nigger a nigger," he barks out, "and they're going to answer to me!"

Thanks, Sarge. But he scares the fuck out of the kids, and they're respectful after that.

It's the early 1960s. Vietnam is starting to ramp up. Black kids die by the dozens over there. Pretty soon it will be by the hundreds, finally by the thousands. My sergeant attaches me to a new unit.

Airbone.

"You black motherfucker," he says, "we're going to throw you out of an airplane!"

In the Army now: Me in civilian clothes when I am in the service in Germany

Airborne means combat. Combat means death.

Hambone saves me once again. I win a base talent contest with the same hambone routine I do in the movie theaters of Oakland. Suddenly I'm part of an army entertainment troupe that tours all over Germany.

Dancing for my supper is something I get used to. But the U.S. Army is the only force that is evil and fucked-up enough to make me dance for my life. I get through my two-year hitch with enough hard-won experience to know what the acronym FTA means when, years later in 1972, I join an anti-war comedy troupe with the name FTA.

Fuck the Army.

The military machine vomits me back onto the streets of Oakland. I am right back where I started.

I'm going out with a girl who works at a North Beach bar that used to be called Mona's and now is called Ann's 440 Club, at 440 on Broadway off the Embarcadero. Later on, Ann's is a beatnik place. But when I go there, it is catering to tough butch lesbians and their femme girlfriends.

Ann Dee, the big, blowsy blond lady who runs it, is really Angela DeSpirito, a singer. She has acts on the club's small stage, singers mostly—Johnny Mathis gets his start there—but some comics, too.

I visit my girlfriend one night while she's waitressing at Ann's. I want to make sure none of the butches misunderstand and think that she is available.

I get struck by lightning as I sit at the bar.

Not literally, of course. It's just that there's a stand-up comic that night who's doing his act. His name is Lenny Bruce, and he is already doing the riff that is going to get him busted.

To *is a preposition and* come *is a verb. I've heard these two words my whole life. As a kid when my folks thought I was sleeping. "Didja come? Huh? Didja? I came, did you come?"*

I stumble out of Ann's a changed man. I have always been funny. There is no way that I could grow up in the Ealy family without learning how to make people laugh. But what Lenny does is something new. He talks onstage like the people around me talk in real life. Plus his laughs have bite. His routines have switchblades concealed inside them.

I am not going to tell you that I see Lenny Bruce and right away chart my course in life. But he infects me with the virus that night at Ann's.

Later on I'm in the audience with George Carlin at the Jazz Workshop show where Lenny gets arrested for obscenity for the first time, for doing the same "didja come?" routine and also for saying "Cocksucker" in public. That switchblade is so sharp it sometimes cuts the person who holds it. For refusing to tell the police his name, Carlin goes to jail, too, in solidarity with Lenny. For all his obscenity raps and lefty political riffs, the one thing the mainstream hates about Lenny is he puts race out there in public. He knew that would get them, and it did.

I start to see all the stand-up I can. Mort Sahl and Woody Allen come through town and perform at the hungry i. A local guy named Ronnie Schell does his act at smaller clubs. Carlin is just starting to happen. He's a little older than I am, but he and I bond over his days in the air force stationed in my old hometown of Shreveport.

Suddenly, black comics are breaking out into the mainstream. I make pilgrimages to see Dick Gregory, Bill Cosby, and Godfrey Cambridge, as well as legendary acts such as the great Moms Mabley and Redd Foxx.

I'm young and brimming with arrogance. I figure if they can do it, so can I. I help found a black improv group that we eventually call the Yankee Doodle Bedbugs. We perform anywhere, in the back rooms of bars, in small clubs, in living rooms.

Improv is the most exhilarating and terrifying thing I ever do. I am up there on a tightrope without a net. It doesn't help that we do outrageous political comedy.

One of our Bedbug routines is my old youthful fantasy, riffing on how it would be if black people took over. We have the African-American Gestapo going door to door. We have Sammy Davis, Jr., hiding Britt Ekland in the basement as though she is Anne Frank.

Again, just like in the hambone dance contests, I kill. The Yankee Doodle Bedbugs are like a black version of the Committee, years before the Committee improv group ever forms up in North Beach. I learn once again that applause is love.

I get the itch, and there's only one place I can go to scratch it.

Hollywood.

Joe Gilbert and Eddie Brown are in the same class as me at Berkeley High. They are the best singers in school. Joe has a pretty tenor and Eddie is lower, like a baritone. They harmonize on gospel songs. Everybody likes them.

I connect with them because Joe is a transplant from Louisiana just like me. The Louisiana-to-Berkeley mafia. You can tell if a person has Louisiana roots because he will pronounce the name of the state in three syllables, as if it's the name of a slutty girl: "Loose Anna."

At the Berkeley High talent show that I organize as a blow against segregated drama department school plays, Joe and Eddie do a version of an old spiritual. "There's a meeting here tonight/There's a meeting here tonight/I can tell by your friendly face/That there's a meeting here tonight."

I think it is the corniest shit I have ever heard, but after the audience votes, they come in first place. Joe and Eddie start to appear at clubs like the hungry i and the Purple Onion. The North Beach beatniks snap their fingers and eat it up.

The folk-song movement is gaining momentum. A group called the Weavers hits the top ten by doing an old Lead Belly song called "Goodnight, Irene." That wakes everyone up to the commercial possibilities of folk music.

Joe and Eddie do folk versions of black spirituals, as well as all-out Weavers-style folkie stuff like the Jewish army marching song "Tzena, Tzena, Tzena." Believe me, you haven't had your head twisted around like it twists when you hear a couple of black dudes from the South singing their hearts out in Hebrew.

Joe is a lot like Richard Pryor. The same crazy energy, the same complexion, the same ugly-cute looks. Women love them some Joe Gilbert. The late 1960s are probably the only days in the history of the world when singing a folk song can get you laid.

I am always hanging out at Joe and Eddie's shows, partly because they are my friends and partly because their gigs attract hippie women who believe in free love. One night Joe and Eddie get me drunk and lure me up onstage.

It's my first solo stand-up comedy routine ever, the first one I do in public anyway, not counting just standing around the kitchen table as a kid cracking up the Ealy household. As it turns out, not a word out of my mouth that evening is mine.

I am so blitzed and so unprepared that I go on autopilot. I do Ronnie Schell's whole act, practically word for word. Same jokes, same patter, everything. I pop my stand-up cherry with another man's dick. If Ronnie's in the audience, I get sued.

But he's not, and I don't. I even get a few laughs.

Ronnie Schell goes on from the San Francisco stand-up scene to play Corporal Duke Slater, Jim Nabors's pussy-hound barracks mate in *Gomer Pyle, U.S.M.C.* I catch a glimpse of him on Nick at Nite or TV Land, and I still feel guilty.

Joe and Eddie are all excited that night because there is an agent in the audience who tells them he'll see their act again if they come to Los Angeles. If he likes it the second time around, he says, he'll see what he can do for them.

They head to L.A. the same week. The agent likes them

fine. Doug Weston of the Troubadour schedules them. It looks as though they are on their way. But the agent asks, "That comic I saw you with, what about him? Where's Mooney?"

"We can get him down here, no problem," Joe says hurriedly. He and Eddie head back up to Oakland to pack up their things and move south. They call me up and tell me I have to come to Los Angeles with them.

We hatch a plan. I am hot for Hollywood. We'll all go together, we decide, three Berkeley High kids busting out of their hometown and into show business. We will road-trip south in my baby blue 1959 Bonneville convertible, tailfins sweeping off the back like a Cadillac. I name the car Hilda, and Hilda will take us to L.A.

It is spring 1963. Gregory Peck wins an Oscar for his portrayal of Atticus Finch in *To Kill a Mockingbird*. Bull Connor is spraying black kids with high-pressure fire hoses in Birmingham. Lee Harvey Oswald is back in the United States from the Soviet Union and makes his first assassination attempt, shooting and missing a U.S. Army major general named Edwin Walker. Next time around, on a Friday in November in Dallas, he'll have some help.

This drive is the flip side of the L.A.-to-Oakland trip Richard Pryor and I will make six years later. I steer Hilda south onto Interstate 5, Oakland to L.A. I have luggage piled up in the front passenger's seat beside me.

In the backseat, Joe and Eddie harmonize, running through their entire repertoire of folk songs. They ain't a-gonna study war no more. They are breaking rocks on the chain gang. They are poor boys being ruined in the house of the rising sun. "I done laid around, and played around/In this ole town too long."

Even though the thought of strangling Joe and Eddie occurs to me more than once over the course of the ten-hour trip, I'm feeling too happy. My whole life, I've been heading for Hollywood. I'm weightless, driving through the California night in a convertible. Free.

I know now that I probably should not have been so serene. Given the immense scale of racism and the depths of bigotry that I encounter in Hollywood, I should have come to town packing a little more heat than a backseat folk duo.

HOLLYWOOD

I always depend on the kindness of women. In Los Angeles, my half sister Carol and I rent a two-bedroom bungalow in a run-down motel on Sunset. The wrong end of Sunset, far away from the Strip.

Carol is doing wigs, huge creations that turn heads. She already knows everybody in town. She is good friends with Tammi Terrell, the singer. A Philly girl, not even twenty when I meet her, she's a slip of a thing with a big childlike eyes and a bigger voice.

Tammi makes her first record when she is sixteen years old. She keeps on getting "discovered," first by James Brown and then, later on, by Berry Gordy, Jr., who pairs her in a series of duets with Marvin Gaye doing Ashford & Simpson songs. When I meet her, she has only a few years to live. She'll be dead from a brain tumor by the end of the decade.

At the bungalow, she's just Tammi, just another one of Carol's friends. Our place is a clearinghouse for black acts passing through Hollywood. They all crash with us. I remember coming in late one night and finding Gladys

Knight's brother and cousins snoring on the floor of our living room.

Bubba Knight and cousins Langston George, Ed Patten, and Bill Guest are the Pips, Gladys's backup singers. They are just coming off their R&B hits "Every Beat of My Heart" and "Letter Full of Tears," but they still have to crash on the floor with friends.

Midnight train: Me and Gladys Knight, but without the Pips

Gladys is off having babies in Atlanta. The Pips are touring on their own. That's the glamorous life of musicians for you.

I wake up early the next afternoon to the sounds of the Pips harmonizing. "Every beat of my heart/Tears me further apart."

It's Joe and Eddie all over again. At least it's R&B and not folk music.

Carol and I make rent any which way we can. We are always scrambling. I take a job selling shoes at the Joseph Magnin department store. A blond girl named Candy Marer works there, too. She is always getting visits from this pop-eyed geek with a watery mouth. He looks like a rickety Ichabod Crane.

"Candy, who's that ugly-ass old man who is always visiting you?" I ask.

She's affronted. "I'm going to marry that ugly-ass old man," she huffs. She does, and she becomes Candy Spelling, wife of Aaron Spelling, the most successful TV producer ever.

Diane DeMarko, the Global sisters, Alice—everybody comes down from the Bay Area to try to make it in L.A. We're all taking odd jobs, going to auditions, tearing ass out to nightclubs every evening. We should have been a dance crew—Mooney and the Killer Women.

Hollywood isn't a late-night town. Everyone always has early calls. But I'm so young that I can dance all night and then show up at an audition looking fresh as a daisy. I'm the first one of the crew to break through.

It's not much, just a commercial for Vote toothpaste, a brand that's now long gone. "Vote for Vote," I say, and flash my pearly whites. I keep my teeth white by not bullshitting but by keeping it real. It pays off. I remember my first royalty paycheck of $56. It doesn't sound like much, but back then the monthly rent on the two-bedroom bungalow on Sunset is $75.

All we have to do is make enough to pay for the phone and the rent. We can go without food. We live on air. We don't care about eating.

The stand-up itch still burns my jock, so I scratch it by auditioning for the Second City improv group touring company. I do some of my Yankee Bedbug stuff, and they like it, and suddenly I'm in.

The first member of the company I get to know is Peter Boyle. *Everybody Loves Racism*—I mean, *Everybody Loves*

Raymond's Peter Boyle. I tell people that I go back so far in Hollywood that I know Peter Boyle when he has hair. I'm back on the improv tightrope. *Chico and the Man*'s Avery Shreiber is in the company with us, and the three of us do a lot of skits together.

Second City doesn't pay, so I run away and join the circus. Literally. The Gatti-Charles Circus advertises for a ringmaster. I don't hesitate. I don't ask myself if I even know what a ringmaster does. It's money, so I call the number and sweet-talk them on the phone.

They are surprised when I show up. I guess I didn't sound black on the telephone. But they get over their shock, and I become the world's first black circus ringmaster.

The best thing about the gig is the costume. I wear a tight pink jacket with brass buttons, cut like an English fox-hunting coat. I get my breeches a size too small so they are tighter than tight, and I polish my thigh-high boots to a sheen. The whole package is finished off with a satin top hat. Step right up! Once again, I am styling! I wish Mama could see me now.

We start in Southern California, then tour east to Arizona, Oklahoma, and Texas. Gatti-Charles is the creation of a furry mustache that masquerades as a man. Its name is Major Gatti. He is one of those honorary majors, just like Colonel Tom Parker, Elvis's manager, is an honorary colonel.

The circus is small, not three-ring but one ring. Gatti pulls together all the animals from popular TV shows and movies. That's the draw. The lions from *Daktari*. Peggy, the chimp from *Bedtime for Bonzo*. Bamboo Harvester, the palomino that played *Mister Ed*. We have everyone but Lassie.

At least, Major Gatti says the animals are movie stars. Who knows if they are or not? It's not like we are going to check hoofprints to see if they are the real thing.

I don't have many dealings with the stock. I look the elephants in the eye and I instantly see that they know what's going on. They know they're slaves.

Back then I don't know shit about Indian or African elephants. I look Jumbo in the eye and I say, "We come from the same place, Africa." I say, "Only a white man could look at you and think, 'Circus,' or 'Theme park.'"

White men always like to ride. They like to believe they are born in the saddle. Down in San Diego at SeaWorld, they ride killer whales. "Weeee-haaaaa!"

I find riding animals about as sporting as shooting fish in a barrel.

Watching how the white handlers act with the animals in the circus makes me think they're all crazy. They will stick their heads in a lion's mouth. I'm thinking, *Is that some freak shit, or what?* Always trying to control what shouldn't be controlled. The white man's motto: Must control everything—always.

I hate how they treat the beasts to get them to do their tricks. It's Dick Cheney–style torture. It's inhumane. To this day, I can never see a circus as entertainment. I know too much.

The handlers can never control the chimps, though, not Peggy and her nasty gang of thugs. *Fuck you,* I can imagine the chimps saying, *I ain't gonna do nothing you tell me, I'm free, white, and twenty-one.* (Now isn't that a real classic American saying?)

The chimps never do the same action twice. They are totally unpredictable. The wind changes direction and suddenly they are going crazy. Like Travis the Chimp, who does commercials and *The Maury Povich Show* and then chews a woman's face off in Connecticut.

The circus band that accompanies all of the acts consists of a dozen drunks with a collection of travel-battered horns and drums. At unexpected points during the show, they abruptly launch into "God Bless America." It happens again and again, but I never know when to expect it. I learn to bribe them so they don't interrupt my act.

All I really have to do as ringmaster is what I am born to do: stand up in front of a crowd and look pretty. I play to the "blues," which is circus-speak for the bleachers. I make corny jokes ("Any palomino is a pal of mine-o") and do routines during the act changes. I lift some of my old Bedbug material, modifying it to suit the occasion.

"These animals are smart, aren't they? What if they take over the earth? Then we'd have animal army soldiers knocking down our doors, keeping all the humans in line. Lassie would have to hide Timmy in the basement and bring him table scraps!"

Gatti-Charles makes the circus of Hollywood, when I get back to it, seem almost sane. I'm back in auditionland again. I get so I can judge just by walking into an audition if the producers are going to be color-blind. Not many of them are. If they aren't, I turn around and walk right back out.

Through Carol I meet a girl who I can tell is interested in me. Yvonne is very pretty and almost as tall as I am. The problem is that she's sixteen, just turning seventeen. I decide I have to wait. I go back and forth to Oakland few times, run off and join the circus again, do improv and work salesman jobs. All the while I am expecting Carol to inform me that Yvonne has found someone else and gotten married.

Only it never happens.

The year she turns eighteen, Yvonne and I are married. I know I can't stay in the bungalow crash palace anymore. I am a married man now, and I have to provide for my beautiful woman. I find a love nest for us on Hancock Place and swear that I am turning my back on Hollywood forever.

That lasts for all of a month. Our honeymoon an idyll. All too soon, we are back in the swirl. Yvonne, Carol, and I host a party at the place on Sunset, the one where a twisted imp I just met asks if I want to have an orgy.

CHAPTER 12

When I first meet Richard, before we ever go to Berkeley together, he's still hanging with his then-wife, Shelley Bonus. Shelley is his second wife out of six or seven or seventeen or a hundred (Richard is a marrying fool).

I like Shelley because she's a dancer, a crazy hippie girl with a huge head of curly hair. Big cyes, bigger breasts—a Jewish Cher. I always call her the White Lady, though she hates it when I do. It makes Richard cackle. Maybe he laughs *because* she hates it.

They hooked up on the set of a movie called *Wild in the Streets*. It's Richard's first movie. Shelley Winters, one of the most cock-hungry actresses in Hollywood, gives him a job. Richard is happy to pay the price of admission to Winters. They get wild in the sheets.

It's the first time I encounter Richard's Hollywood jones. He wants to be a movie star more than anything. He grows up idolizing John Wayne. Give Richard the choice between being a stand-up star and a movie star, and he goes for the Hollywood bullshit every time.

The other Shelley, Shelley Bonus, is a hippie chick extra in *Wild in the Streets,* and Richard has a small part. He gets them to hire me to do all his stunts.

During the shoot, Richard and I encounter set decorators on the crew who are spraying a liquid substance on the streets to make them look like it has just rained.

"What's that stuff?" Richard asks.

"It's called 'nigger-size,'" the union guys tell him, not even bothering to notice if we're offended.

"Nigger-size?" I ask, incredulous.

"Yeah, it's what we nigger-size the streets with," the crew explains. Richard and I look at each other and shake our heads. It's 1968 in Los Angeles, but it may as well be 1920 in the Deep South.

Richard's wife, Shelley, is Hollywood, even if she comes from New York. Her daddy is Danny Kaye's manager. Daddy gives his daughter a typical L.A. gift—a $40,000 Maserati. This drives Richard crazy. He hates the car because he didn't buy it. I wind up hiding it in the driveway of my house in the Exposition Hills.

Richard and Shelley have a child, Rain. Richard is big on fathering children but not too keen on behaving like a father. He and Shelley alternate between knockdown, drag-out fights and flower-child dreamy-ass shit. I see them out in the yard of their house in Beverly Hills, and the two of them are literally hugging trees and kissing rocks.

"You see this rock?" Richard says to me. "Its name is Forgotten. We named it. We named a motherfucking rock, man."

For a little while it's Yvonne and me and Shelley and Richard. We go around on double dates, like white people. Richard is a drinker and Yvonne and I don't put anything like that into our bodies. We are the odd couples.

Dressed to the nines: Yvonne and me ready for a night out

Right after they have Rain, we have our first child, a boy, who we call Shane. Rain and Shane. They're born six months apart. Yvonne has her baby shower at Richard's. Later on we have a girl and name her Spring. Every summer I bring Daryl and Duane to live with us, and have Lisa down from Oakland, too. Yvonne is a great stepmom to them all. They adore her.

In his stand-up during this time, Richard doesn't talk as much about black and white as he does about men and women. Or pricks and pussies. Or bitches and sons-of-bitches.

I got a wife, and it's really funny to have a wife, man, because we were in love like a bitch until we got married. It's true. We used to have fun things to do together. I used to bring her a rock, and she'd go, "Oh! A rock! A rock, for me?" Now it's more like, how big is that rock that she hit me with?

For a little while Yvonne and I live in the guesthouse Shelley and Richard fix up behind their house. We sit there and listen to the two of them fight in the big house. They rattle the walls.

Most artists aren't good with day-to-day business. The more talented the artist, the higher the level of insanity, like Van Gogh. Richard doesn't cash his paychecks. He leaves money around the house. When he gets tired of driving a car, he parks it on the street and just leaves it. Shelley does the same thing. Practicality ain't a strong suit for either one of them.

Richard burns to be a movie star. "Mr. Mooney, I want to be an actor," he says to me, over and over again. He's always doubting himself. He's like a little kid, needing to be reassured. "What do you think, Paul? Do you think I can be an actor?"

"Oh, yeah," I say. "You're the best actor."

"I am?" Richard says.

"You got everybody convinced you're not crazy," I say, laughing. "That's the best acting job I've ever seen."

Richard decides that if Hollywood won't make a film with him as the star, he will do it himself. Richard's film *Bon Appétit* is a project conceived and executed in a drug haze. The plot centers on a black man accused of raping a white woman. Richard doesn't plan out the movie. He just buys an expensive 16mm movie camera and simply starts filming.

The script is handwritten in a spiral notebook with torn pages, but no one pays any attention to it.

At different times, *Bon Appétit* is called *Uncle Tom's Fairy Tales* and *The Trial*. Richard is helpless to finish it. The story changes so often that no one can follow the action. He hires a twenty-three-year-old UCLA film student named Penelope Spheeris to make sense of the reels and reels of footage he has shot.

Spheeris tries. She actually moves into the house with Richard, Shelley, and baby Rain in order to work on editing the raw material. But it's an impossible task. *Bon Appétit* never does get released. Penelope Spheeris goes on to be a big film director, making *Wayne's World*.

Another big idea, lost in the haze. With all the cocaine he's doing, Richard's mind jumps from subject to subject like one of those Mexican beans with worms inside them.

Whenever I read reviews about what a comic genius Richard is, I have the same response: I know him too well. Yeah, Richard Pryor is the funniest man America has ever seen. (Mark Twain is runner-up. Richard is Dark Twain.) But I know he is a junkie first, and a genius second. That's cold, but it's the hard, sad truth. It's the reality of Richard's life, but not many of his idolizers want to hear that shit. It's the fundamental, up-front thing you have to say about him. You talk about genius afterward.

When you're as tight with someone as I am with Richard, you can't avoid his faults. You can't gloss over them. Critics and commentators who look from a distance at Richard the movie star–comedian–celebrity can do that. I'll never have a closer friend than Richard. I don't love him because he's a comic genius, and I don't hate him because he is a degenerate drug user. I love him because he's Richard.

Best friends: Richard and Yvonne

Around this time I meet another Carol—Carol Brooker, a beautiful girl from Chicago. Carol B. shows up in Los Angeles with a huge natural. It stops traffic. No one has ever seen a huge Afro like that. Her hair must be three feet wide. She has to go through doors sideways.

Carol B. becomes our style maven. She's like Mr. Black-well, telling us what's in and out. She sits down in front of the makeup mirror and doesn't get up for three hours. But when she does, she looks wonderful.

We all stay in a big duplex at Highland and Wilshire. When the rent collectors come around, we pretend we live in the apartment next door. They knock on one door of the duplex, we answer the other. "Oh, those people? They're in Europe."

We don't have any money, but we do have style. Carol B. makes sure of that. The first time I get a pair of platform shoes, I head over to see Richard. He can't figure out what's different.

"You are always smaller than me, motherfucker," he says. "What the fuck did you do, grow?"

I lift up my bells and show Richard my snakeskin platforms. He goes nuts. "Oh, man, we are going to go get mine tomorrow."

Pretty soon, everybody is wearing them. We always call them "Crenshaw pumps." I see Jim Brown in a pair of platforms, a big 275-pound man teetering along in heels. Everybody's walking around like they're just in from planet Jupiter. The world slides off the deep end. People don't dress, they *costume*. Richard grows a natural, the kind of big, Wookie-ass 'do that everybody back then calls a "freedom cap." I develop a theory that the wilder the times, the more whack the outfits. The bigger the social upheaval—and the 1960s is the biggest—the crazier the clothes. The style fits the scene.

CHAPTER 13

The late 1960s are confused. Nobody knows how to act. The old white folks in showbiz suddenly see blue jeans and black people where before there were only tuxedos and black waiters. They don't know what to make of it all.

In 1969, Jim Brown and Raquel Welch perform Hollywood's first acknowledged interracial love scene in a movie called *100 Rifles*. James Earl Ray retracts his bogus guilty plea in the assassination of Martin Luther King, Jr., but the government conspiracy to kill America's greatest prophet is covered up. John Lennon and Yoko Ono do their "bed-in" for peace in Montreal, and everyone is singing their antiwar anthem, "Give Peace a Chance."

The old-style Hollywood club at that time is Villa Capri, really just an Italian restaurant that Frank Sinatra makes famous. Musty, traditional places such as Chasen's still reserve booths for people like Ron and Nancy. Some joints are still "jacket-and-tie only." But movie-studio Hollywood is on its last legs.

Black power, psychedelia, and the Sunset Strip scene blow that antiquated shit straight out of the water. Most of the new clubs are democratic, like Luau, the Troubadour, or the Cheetah out in Santa Monica. Anyone can go there, dressed any old which way.

But a few private clubs spring up, ones that mix the old style of exclusivity with the new style of anything goes. One of them is the Daisy, with a snooty, beautiful hostess that Richard is always trying to fuck. She won't have anything to do with him.

But the club we wind up going to, and the one that puts me in the middle of the Hollywood swirl, is called the Candy Store. A Frenchman named Jean Chicot runs it. It is a real private club in the sense that you have to be a member to get in. Why am I not surprised when I learn that only white folks are members?

We don't set out trying to do it, but we wind up integrating the Candy Store.

Los Angeles is the bourgeois town of all bourgeois towns, a vile, racist city from the very start. It's always been way more conservative than people think. Hollywood folks like to believe they are wrapped in their liberal beliefs, but it's all just a ruse. They got the complexion for the protection. Hollywood only brings up race when it works for them.

Down in Orange County, they are right-wing and racist and proud of it. I actually prefer that to the bullshit pretense of being open-minded in Hollywood. In Orange County, at least I know where I stand—on a stool with a noose around my neck. Up north in movieland, I am always getting side-swiped by prejudice, because everyone assumes their racial shit is all settled, when it most definitely is not.

The Candy Store gives the white, uptight Hollywood establishment a controlled environment to taste the hippie shit and the racial shit that is happening down on the Strip. It features only female DJs playing Motown, the Doors, the

Byrds, Arthur Lee and Love. The Candy Store is Peter Lawford's club, and Sinatra comes in with Mia Farrow.

My friend Diane DeMarko works the door, so we have no problem getting in. But it's a white bastion. The staff is all white. Chicot probably doesn't think about it much, but he has only white waitresses and staffers.

One evening Yvonne and I are in the Candy Store early, visiting with Diane. Chicot is freaking out because one of his waitresses doesn't show up.

Diane says, "Yvonne is a waitress." Chicot looks over to see this stunning black woman sitting with me.

He gives Yvonne a uniform and she works the whole night. At the end of it, Chicot is so thankful I think he is going to kiss her.

"You saved us tonight," he says, and he gives Yvonne a job.

After that, the Candy Store becomes our playpen. I'm there every night on the dance floor, a tall, handsome black guy with movie-star looks. Chicot finally realizes that I hip up the place. I'm an asset, where before he saw me only as a nuisance.

It's my first big, concentrated dose of Hollywood celebrity. One of those whiplash places, where people are always jerking their heads around, rubber-necking. Is that . . . ?

Yes, it is. It's Racquel Welch, Barbra Streisand, Shelley Winters, Lana Turner, Ava Gardner, Jane Fonda, Mick Jagger, John Lennon, Ringo Starr. The big TV stars of the day, *My Favorite Martian*'s Bill Bixby, *Ben Casey*'s Vince Edwards, and *The Man from U.N.C.L.E.*'s Robert Vaughn.

I don't get starstruck. Mama's ironclad rule that nobody is better than me prevents that. Except for once, in the Candy Store, the first time I sit at the same table as Elizabeth Taylor.

I am tongue-tied. She is such an icon in my life. Sitting there in person, at a banquette in this little private club in Beverly Hills, she exudes such class. She doesn't show skin. Yet she is the sexiest person alive. In terms of sex appeal, Liz Taylor can school the young tramps who dress like hookers today.

The Candy Store is like that. Close Encounters with the Rich and Famous. I tell Ava Gardner that she should write a book about Frank Sinatra. She looks up at me with those wonderful eyes of hers and coos, "I don't kiss and tell. What's between Frank Sinatra and me is between Frank Sinatra and me." Not nasty, but firm.

Mia Farrow is complaining that they won't let her out of her *Peyton Place* TV contract to let her go do a movie in New York—*Rosemary's Baby*. This is back before her radical transformation, when she still has beautiful long hair down to her ass.

"Just leak it that you are going out with me," I say to her. "They'll let you out of your contract right away."

Sinatra isn't with her that night. She does go to New York to have her demon baby, and the film producers make her cut her hair. She looks like a little boy. Frank's furious. Things aren't the same with them after that.

At the Candy Store, I fit in. I get the first real hint of how I strike people, that combination of fascination and terror that I encounter again and again in my life. Ann-Margret flits through the club and recognizes me from *Dance Party*.

"You made it!" she says. Everywhere she goes, that woman is like a blast of freshness and energy.

I don't feel like I've made it. The Candy Store is like a golden womb, private, intimate, where everyone knows everybody else. I love it when I'm there. But I never forget that outside the doors of that little club it's Hollywoodland, where I can't get my foot in the door.

I'm still living on the edge. I don't have a dime. Professionally, I'm not even showing up yet on Hollywood's radar screen. But I love to dance, and that's what I'm doing every night at the Candy Store among all the pretty people.

Maybe I'm window dressing. I don't care. I'm seeing and being seen, becoming known. That's vital in Hollywood. People need to see you around, check you out, before you'll be accepted as a member of the club. They don't like strangers in that town. What town does?

Richard fits in at the Candy Store, too. At that point, he isn't real famous. But he has a buzz around him. He is one more Hollywood hotshot among the stars at the Candy Store. They accept that he should be there, walking among them. He doesn't have to dance for his supper the way I do.

He is just coming off one of his appearances on *The Ed Sullivan Show*. That's about as big as a comic can get as far as national recognition goes. From there it's albums, it's headlining in comedy clubs, it's Vegas. That's the dream path of comedy back then.

Sullivan is a stiff, no-talent guy who used to be a gossip columnist. He invites Richard on his show to do his safe, bland, Cosby-style routines. The physical gag about the bowling pin, stuff like that. Sullivan likes him so much that he has him on a half dozen times.

They like Richard in New York. He goes on *The Tonight Show,* when it's still broadcast out of the city, before it moves to Burbank, California. Merv Griffith has him on, too.

All this recognition in New York works its magic in Hollywood, where people are like sheep. They have to be told it's okay to like somebody. Once they're told, they fall into line meekly. Baa-baaa.

So when Richard comes to the Candy Store with me,

people know him. The two of us, him in the lead, me following behind. I get a glimpse of Hollywood power. The crowd parts. Everyone is looking at us. It's heady and intoxicating, but I have an impulse to reject it, too.

We pass by Steve McQueen. He lets Richard go by, but then stops me. "Hey, that looks just like Richie Pryor."

That's what people call him back then. Richie Pryor, or even Dick Pryor.

"You look just like Steve McQueen," I say, and follow Richard to a booth.

In 1970, one of the biggest stars on TV is a black man. *The Flip Wilson Show* is top-rated. Flip performs in the round, with the audience seated on all sides. When I ask him why, he says, "That way they can't corner me."

Richard and I see Flip all the time at the Candy Store. He hires Richard to write for him and appear in sketches on the program. George Carlin works as a writer on Flip's show, too.

Flip does characters, the kind of stuff that Richard can see himself doing, only it's got a softer edge. Like Reverend Leroy, preacher at the Church of What's Happening Now. His most popular character is a drag act, Geraldine, with her line, "The devil made me do it."

It gives us hope that the devil can make us do it, too. If he can make it, we can make it. Flip comes to the Candy Store and people fawn over him, the big star. Then he and Richard go out and score blow. Richard works on Flip's show and Flip's snow at the same time.

Flip has an eighteen-year-old white girl, Amy, who acts as a drug mule. She goes out and buys dope for him. Richard poaches her. He steals Flip's drug courier from him. Amy starts muling for Richard. Flip flips. He never forgives Richard.

Billy Dee Williams comes into the Candy Store, too. He looks me up and down and says, "If I had your looks, I'd be a real movie star." He wants to meet Richard, but he doesn't want to be seen with him. He's under the Motown protection plan, and Richard has a wild reputation. Billy Dee's a real prima donna. He won't go out with us. He thinks we're too wild, that we might get him in trouble with his Motown handlers.

Richard loves the whole scene. I mean, he really loves the glamourous life of Hollywood. More than the money, I think, more than the pussy even, more than everything but the drugs, Richard Pryor loves him some Hollywood star power. He could give a lot of it up and just be satisfied alone in a room with a base pipe, but he'd miss that Hollywood connection too much.

Yet giving it up is what he's always filling my ear about back then. In the middle of the Candy Store, which in Richard Pryor's eyes is like a slice of heaven, he's talking about giving it up. How he hates it. Sullivan and Griffin and *The Tonight Show*. The Las Vegas clubs and the top billing.

"It ain't me, Paul," he says. "I can't even say the motherfucking word *bullshit*! I can't say *ass*!"

I want to respond, "Look, I see the way your face lights up when Steve McQueen recognizes you." But I don't. I know that these people, the ones we are sitting among at the Candy Store, are the same ones who think they can tell Richard Pryor what to say, how to behave, who to be. To tell him he can't say "ass" or "bullshit."

He is a man all torn apart. Hollywood is telling him, You can have everything you want, but we have to put you through our deflavorizer first.

What Richard wants is what I want, what everyone in the

world wants. To be accepted, to be loved for who we are, not for some playacting phony version of ourselves.

That's what he and I set out to do over the next few years: conquer Hollywood on our own terms. Our first step is to turn our backs on it entirely and make our Motown drive north in a blue Buick convertible, heading for the wilds of Berkeley.

CHAPTER 14

The stretch in Berkeley is Richard's time in the wilderness. He's like Jesus, going out into the desert and meeting the devil. For Richard, the devil takes the form of a white powder from Bolivia. And unlike Jesus, Richard doesn't conquer his devil. He makes friends with it.

Richard cannot stay in Berkeley if it's a dry town. Luckily for him, the Bay Area is a big port of entry, with freighters docking every day, many of them with kilos of cocaine hidden in their holds. He finds it just as easy to score in Berkeley as he did in L.A. In that sense, at least, all is right with Richard's world.

He holes up in a shitty little studio apartment on the west side, near the marina. The interstate pounds by within shouting distance. He loves it. It's like he's denying himself for the sake of his art. His job, as he sees it, is to find a way out of the box that white people want to keep him in.

The fundamental truth about Richard during his year in the Berkeley wilderness is that he's sick to death of white folks, white jive, white culture. He feels like it's killing him. He has to get out from under it just to survive as a man. It's his "fuck it all" period.

I bring him by to meet Mama. He loves the fact that she steadfastly remains at 18th Street, in the middle of the Oakland ghetto. Mama likes Richard. She fixes him my favorite dish, neck bones and butter beans.

"Those are the best neck bones I ever ate," he says.

Mama thinks he's fooling with her, but he's not. That meal isn't the first beef neck bones Richard eats in his life. His grandfather, just like Daddy Preston, is a hunter. He and I are raised by our grandparents in similar households, but in totally different circumstances.

As a child, Richard has a much harder time of it. He's not in a warm, protected environment of family, like I am. He gets molested when he's five years old. He's got all the brothel bullshit to put up with.

But he chows down on possum, rabbit, whistle pig, fatback, garden greens, and chitterlings like the best of us. Black folks develop a taste for food like this in slave times. The massa always takes the choice cuts for himself. We are left with the snouts, ears, neck bones, feet, rectums, and intestines. But we make a silk purse out of a sow's ear. The discarded cuts turn out to be the best eating.

Richard recognizes Mama and Daddy instantly. From his childhood, they are familiar figures to him. He grows up along the Chicago River, a tributary on one end of the Mississippi River, just like I grow up along the Red River, a tributary on the other end. It's like we are twins from different families.

The main difference is Richard needs more love than I do. He needs assurance. He's vulnerable. I get so much love from

Mama growing up that I am set for life. So I don't need to look for approval so much. I am self-contained. Richard isn't, and that's the source of a lot of trouble and a lot of good at the same time.

I hold on to who I am. When you know who you are, it's harder for people to fuck with you. Hollywood is dangerous because the great hobby they have in that town is fucking with other people. Building you up, knocking you down, until finally you are destroyed. They all want to create you and mold you.

Richard and I talk about *Frankenstein* all the time. We are always riffing on the old movie, because we know that Hollywood has the Frankenstein syndrome. Just like Dr. Frankenstein, producers want to stitch together body parts and build their own stars, their own monsters. If you don't watch out in this town, you wind up with someone else's dick attached to your crotch.

But just like in the Frankenstein story, the monster always hates the doctor. In the black-and-white original *Frankenstein* movie, the one with Boris Karloff as the monster, the doctor has all the dialogue: "Now I know what it feels like to be God! . . . The brain of a dead man waiting to live again in a body I made with my own hands!"

Dr. Frankenstein talks throughout the whole movie. The monster says only one thing: "Aaaah!" But less is more.

I always thought of Frankenstein's monster as a black man. All the white people are always chasing him. "Get him! Get him!" That crowd of cracker-ass villagers with torches is a lynch mob. The monster runs exactly like the caricature of a black man running from a mob, wild-eyed, grunting like an animal.

"Aaaah!"

The villagers are terrified of him, just like crackers are terrified of the black man ("What's that? Who's out there? Niggerstein! Is it him?") And when they catch him, he whups villager ass, just like a black man. He throws mother-fuckers all over the place.

"Aaaah!"

The thing is, in the movie, all you remember is the monster. Who remembers the doctor? Karloff becomes a big star. But Colin Clive? He stays a nobody.

Hollywood is the Frankenstein story blown up into a whole industry—the movie business.

On the drive up to Berkeley, in between hollering out those Motown songs, Richard tells me that the people around him sometimes appear to him as devils.

"I'm in a meeting down in motherfucking Hollywood, Mr. Mooney, and I ain't kidding, all I see is horns and tails! Really! All these folks around me got cloven feet and forked tongues!"

So while he's in Berkeley, Richard is a Frankenstein's monster who becomes a hermit. Richard goes into that rat hole of an apartment and doesn't come out for a few weeks. He does some surgery on his own ass, cutting off the body parts that Dr. Hollywood grafted onto him.

He's got two things to sustain him—Marvin Gaye and Malcolm X. All he does is listen to music and read Malcolm all day long. That's the winter of "What's Going On," Marvin's masterpiece. Richard has it on his turntable and puts it on repeat. "Mother, mother, there's too many of you crying."

The song is something new out of Motown. It talks about the here and now. I know Marvin really does have a brother in Vietnam. Plus he's sick over the death of Tammi Terrell, the sweet little Philly soul singer who used to hang out at our bungalow on Sunset, gone at age twenty-four. If she'd lived, she'd have been bigger than Whitney, a superstar.

So out of all this pain comes a work of genius. I hear "What's Going On" everywhere, coming out of car radios and stereo speakers. Number one on the R&B charts, of course, but when I look at the pop charts, it's stuck at number two behind this pop number by Three Dog Night called "Joy to the World."

I think, yeah, that figures. "Joy to the World" is catchier than hell, but it ignores what's going on around me on the streets. "Joy to the World" is like everything that Richard is trying to get away from by hiding out in Berkeley. Mindless white-world pop froth. "What's Going On" is everything he's moving toward; genius and keeping it real. But the wider *Billboard* pop-chart world ain't ready to embrace it.

It's maddening. Vegas gatekeepers don't want to hear *bullshit* and *ass* spoken out loud from their stages, much less *nigger* and *motherfucker*. This is what they want: "Joy to the fishes in the deep blue sea/Joy to you and me."

Like I said, catchy song. But it just ain't where our heads are at right at the moment.

I'm staying at Mama's on 18th Street. I go up to Berkeley to check in with Richard every once in a while, make sure he's all right, hasn't lit himself on fire with a base pipe. For a few weeks I'm the only human being he sees outside of food-delivery boys.

"I got to go back to L.A.," I say. Richard is so over L.A. at that moment, he looks at me like I'm saying I have to go visit the twin cities of Sodom and Gomorrah, brush up on my evil.

"You all right?" I ask.

He bristles. "Yeah, man, sure, I'm all right. Why wouldn't I be?"

"Just asking," I say, and I leave Richard in the wilderness and drive down to L.A. I figure my goal now is just to get known. That's how you do it in Hollywood—you get known first and succeed later.

CHAPTER 15

All the while Richard is up north taking his mental-health break from the business, I am going back and forth between Oakland and L.A. Yvonne and I have a house in Hancock Park, an old Los Angeles neighborhood where all the rich people live, only she and I are the exceptions. She's dancing at a strip club for bread, waitressing at the Candy Store, picking up any old job to make the rent. I'm dancing as fast as I can, doing anything for a paycheck.

Everyone falls in love with Yvonne. It's embarrassing. Men see her and trip head over heels for her. It doesn't matter that I'm standing right there, her husband. They still lose their minds.

The first time it happens is with Peter Boyle, my Second City improv partner.

"Hey, honey, what do you do?" Boyle says, practically drooling. "Are you in the movies? You want to be in the movies?"

A time-honored Hollywood opening line. I gently tell

Peter that Yvonne is my wife. "I know that!" he snaps at me. "What's you point?" Being funny.

Warren Beatty sees Yvonne at the Candy Store and chats her up. George Peppard, Elizabeth Ashley's husband, flips over her, sending her roses again and again. He tracks her down at the club where she works. John Barrymore, Jr., Drew's father, follows Yvonne around like a puppy dog. It's like I have to walk around with a stick, just to beat them away.

My cousin Alice, too. She is so pretty it gets her into trouble. Garry Marshall, the director, seems smitten by her. Mickey Rooney bothers her constantly at the Candy Store. "If you won't go out on a date with me, will you at least marry me?" he asks. Alice isn't sure if he's joking, but she's not about to be wife number 1,803 for Mickey Rooney.

"I like to get married early in the morning," Rooney says. "That way, if it doesn't work out, I haven't wasted the whole day."

Alice, Yvonne, Carol, Carol B., Diane DeMarko—we are all doing anything and everything we can to earn money. My agent gets me an audition for a Steve McQueen movie, *The Reivers,* which is based on a William Faulkner novel. *Reiver* is a Southern word I haven't heard since Shreveport. It means what we today would call a player.

They like me in the audition, and I think I'm going to get the role of Ned, a sidekick. I'm young and naive. I don't realize yet that the real business of Hollywood isn't making movies. It's breaking hearts.

They give the part of Ned to a TV actor named Rupert Crosse. He gets nominated for an Academy Award for best supporting actor. He loses to Gig Young in *They Shoot Horses, Don't They?* I'm so disappointed over not getting the part of Ned, I wish somebody'd shoot *me.* I know if I acted in that movie, I'd get nominated, too. But the difference between me and Rupert is I'd win the motherfucking Oscar.

I go on the ABC afternoon show *The Dating Game,* because even though I am married, the producers pay scale. It's okay, because everyone is doing it. Half the people on the show are married or living together. It should be called *The Adultery Game.* When I go on, Yvonne is already pregnant with Shane.

The program's gimmick has a girl asking questions of three guys, who are hidden behind a screen. After she listens to their answers and decides what she thinks of them, she picks the one she wants to date. Tom Selleck goes on *The Dating Game* twice and doesn't get picked either time. Later on, people like Oprah Winfrey and Michael Richards do the show before they are stars. A white-bread DJ named Jim Lange is the host, but the real genius behind *The Dating Game* is Chuck Barris, the same producer who comes up with the ideas for *The Gong Show* and *The Newlywed Game.*

After I appear on the program (I get picked, but the bachelorette and I decide to take the prize money in cash instead of going on a date), I tell Alice she should go on, too. Alice does, has a good time, and gets paid. She's choosing between three black men. Suddenly, when the show airs, Chuck Barris gets a call from an outraged viewer. It's Howard Hughes.

"Why in the hell do you have a white girl on with a bunch of niggers?" Howard screams into the phone.

Barris gently tells Hughes that Alice is black. "She's Creole," Barris says. The world's richest man then meekly does his best Gilda Radner–as–Emily Litella impression: "Never mind."

Howard Hughes shouldn't feel too badly. He's not the first person to get tripped up by Alice, my beautiful cousin who can pass. It can happen to any racist cracker asshole.

The best gig we all get is like a grown-up version of *Dance Party*. Hugh Hefner syndicates a show he calls *Playboy After Dark*, which is him showing off his lifestyle. He sits around the Playboy Mansion in his satin smoking jacket, smoking a pipe.

Hef has a celebrity on, they talk, the celebrity performs, Bunnies walk on and walk off. It's like a talk show with tits, and they need a lot of pretty people to make the Mansion look less like a mausoleum. I'm a regular, and I bring Alice on with me every once in a while. The best part of *Playboy After Dark* is meeting all the talent, people like Linda Ronstadt, Billy Eckstein, Ike and Tina, and Sonny and Cher. There is nowhere else you can find odd-couple pairings like Ronstadt and Billy "Mr. B" Eckstein doing a duet of Billie Holiday's "God Bless the Child."

Meeting talent and dancing. That's what I am there for. I'm stylin' once again. For one set of the show I wear a green knit tunic and a black patent-leather belt. I look like one of Robin Hood's merry men. I bust some moves in front of the biggest acts of the day.

Rock groups such as Canned Heat and Joe Cocker and the Grease Band jam for us in Hefner's "Romper Room." It's like we're in a small, private nightclub. There's a lot funkier music going down at the time, but Hefner's tastes run to the middle of the road, even though he styles himself a hipster.

Hef is a smooth, hepcat presence throughout the taping, with his girlfriend Barbi Benton surgically grafted to his side. Behind her back, everyone calls her "Boobie Benton." With her bubbly attitude, brunette bangs, and glistening lips, she's white-girl sexy. *Playboy* sexy. Girl-next-door sexy. She loves me. Off camera, she seeks me out. She likes me because I tease her and make her laugh. She's the boss man's lady, but I don't care. I catch Hefner watching us, a gleam in his eye, and I think, *That cat would like to watch us do more than just flirt.*

Hefner's taste in comics runs to the middle of the road, too. He has on Jerry Lewis, Sid Caesar, and *F Troop*'s Larry Storch. The great Mort Sahl does an incomprehensible blackboard bit about politics. Hefner also favors the comic Dick Shawn, who is famous from the ensemble comedy movie *It's a Mad, Mad, Mad World.* Shawn's act is pretty bland, but it's got some freaky touches. In his stage act, he doesn't come in from the wings, he emerges from a pile of bricks.

The most memorable thing about Dick Shawn's career is how he left it, dying of a heart attack onstage in San Diego. A real comedian's death. The audience thinks it's part of the act. They don't leave, even after the paramedics take the body away. Sometimes I die onstage with my act, too, but never to that degree.

Once again, on *Playboy After Dark,* I'm wallpaper. Dancing and hanging out. But I do get to hang out at the Playboy Mansion whenever I want. I swim in the grotto. Play pool with Jimmy Caan. Hef runs the place like a club. You can sit down day or night at the dining room table, and a waiter gives you a menu from which you can order.

One time, by mistake, I open the wrong door off a hallway near the dining room. It's a closet filled with Tampax and Kotex and every kind of feminine hygiene product imaginable. The Mansion isn't a house, it's a harem. The women walking around are all brick-shithouse knockouts.

Some of the same group of celebrities that I know from the Candy Store show up at the Mansion. These people are always seeing me around, so they get the idea that I'm in the mix. Even if I'm on *Playboy After Dark* just as a kind of male eye candy, I figure that it's good to get known. Meanwhile, I'm trying to make a name for myself as a comedian. Being part of an improv group like the Yankee Doodle Bedbugs or Second City is one thing. Getting up onstage and flying solo as a stand-up act is another. Improv is great for timing and thinking on your feet. But you're still protected by the other members of the troupe. If you flop, they can step up and cover for you.

I'm born as a stand-up comic in 1970 on the stage of Ye Little Club, Joan Rivers's joint in Beverly Hills. Joan opens the place so she and her comedian friends have a place to try out material. It's small, casual, intimate, a jazz club for jazz people.

The great big-band vocalist Anita O'Day headlines at Ye Little Club. The house singer is my old friend Ann Dee from Ann's 440 Club in San Francisco, where I first see Lenny Bruce. Almost in spite of herself, Joan breaks some big acts. Trini Lopez starts out at Ye Little Club, as does the folk singer Barry McGuire, the "Eve of Destruction" guy.

Getting born ain't a pretty spectacle. It's bloody and messy and there's a lot of screaming and bawling. That's the way it is for me on the stage of Ye Little Club. What's great is that Joan Rivers understands. She has me back again and again. I'm trying out my routines, seeing what works and what doesn't.

My comedy is a nuclear bomb inside my mind. It's a weapon that's never been tested. It just blows up and flattens everybody. I start out talking about the funniest shit I know, which is race.

Thank God, Paul Revere was white, because if he was black, they'd have shot his ass. "He done stole that horse, let's kill him! Kill him!" And who do they say sewed the flag, what's her name? Betsy Ross? Now, come on—they had slaves back then. Betsy Ross was asleep at six. You know some big black mama was up all night sewing that flag! "Honey, oh, Lawd, have mercy, I'm just up so late sewing this flag, I'm seeing stars!" And she's thinking about the stripes on her back, from the whip. So there we get it, the stars and stripes. But as soon as the white men got there, the white lady Betsy Ross jumped up, "See what I did?"

Right away, I notice something. The black people in the audience react to me way differently than the white people. Like in this routine. White people like the killing of the black horse-thief. They like the coon talk of the slave woman.

But the white folks get tight-faced and nervous when I start making fun of the white lady Betsy Ross. I know they like history. White people like going back in time, which is always a problem for me. I can go back only so far. Any farther and my black ass is in chains.

At Ye Little Club, I always drop some history into my act. It's knowledge. There's always a message in my comedy. But it's like a time bomb. The audiences might not get it right away. But they get it later that night, the next day, a week later. Then they understand.

I start to study white audiences. I see their reactions. I get my first walkouts. A lot of white people remind me of scared rabbits. When the wolf comes out, they run. They twitch their little pink noses and haul ass out of there.

When I imitate middle-class white speech, I see a flicker of unease cross the faces of the white people in the audience. Then, when I go into ghetto riff, the smiles return. They're fine as long as I am making fun of the same kind of people they make fun of, chinks and spics and niggers. But as soon as I start talking about them, I can clear a room.

My favorite is Lassie. Is that dog smart? Goddamn that dog is smart. They talk to Lassie like Lassie is a person.

*"Lassie, hey, Lassie, how's your mom? I love you! Call
me in an hour!" I saw one episode, Grandpa has a heart
attack? Lassie drove him to the hospital. And made a
left turn. I said, Goddamn, Lassie, this is a smart dog.
Lassie got other dogs killed. Little ghetto boy, hits his
dog with a hammer, trying to get his dog to do what
Lassie does. "Goddamn, you better talk to me like
Lassie! You don't, I'm going to give you to the Vietnamese family!"*

When I'm up onstage, I'm watching the audience like a
hawk. I'm analyzing little tics, tells, and reactions they don't
even know they are having. I study them. I have jungle eyes,
I don't miss a thing.

I start to get so I can orchestrate my act. Some nights I
feel like I'm Quincy Jones, like I'm playing the white audience like an instrument. *That* line'll make 'em nervous, but
this line'll bring 'em back. I tease it to the edge.

It's funny, isn't it? Most of the white folks at Ye Little
Club laugh about everyone else, but when I talk about them,
they suddenly lose their sense of humor. They freeze up like
an engine out of oil. If I do it enough, if I push it too far for
them, they get up and leave.

So I think, *Fuck them.* I do it more than enough and I
push it too far. Some nights I'm not happy until I provoke a
walkout.

That's when I first find my true audience. Black people,
who are always with me, and brave white people. The non-
rabbits of the bunch. The ones who can laugh at themselves.

What I like about Ye Little Club is nobody ever tells me to
tone it down. I have to give props to Marshal Edgel, who
runs the place, and to Joan Rivers for that. Joan has comedy

in her bones. She knows never to fuck with anyone else's act. Ye Little Club is a free-fire zone. It's like this little oasis of free speech in the middle of the 1970 culture wars. It's not celebrity heavy like the Candy Store. Only the hip people know about it. The wife of the chief of police of Beverly Hills used to be a regular. She was one of my first fans. She used to howl at my routines.

But in those days, no one pays club comics anything. There are a lot of places where comics can go to do stand-up. The Etc. Club, Paradise Gardens, the Gypsy Club, the Bla-Bla Café in Studio City, the Improv on Melrose. But all over, it's the same. You play for no pay. Owners are doing you a favor. The attitude is "Get on television, then come back and we'll talk about paying you."

I'm not on TV yet, except for an uncredited walk-on in one of Richard's projects, a made-for-TV thing called *Carter's Army*. A cracker redneck sergeant commands a platoon of black soldiers. Richard is great as a medic who is scared of his own shadow. I'm one of the soldiers. The gig pays me scale for a few days, and that's worth it for me.

Through James Watson, an actor-comic I grew up with, I get involved in an antiwar improv group that Jane Fonda puts together. It's like a traveling carnival show with politics, organized by a peace activist named Fred Gardner. A folksinger named Len Chandler performs, plus a lesbian singer and actress named Holly Near. We put up a stage near military bases, like the one in South Bay at San Pedro, and play to the troops. There's a lot of antiwar sentiment among the soldiers, so we're a hit. We call ourselves FTA—Fuck the Army.

My life is crazy. I'm working at make-the-rent jobs during the day, gigging at Ye Little Club at night, and then every weekend going out and fucking with the army alongside Jane Fonda. It's funny to work with Jane Fonda, doing

Fuck the Army: Me onstage in the antiwar improv troupe FTA

antiwar theater during the day, and then see her old man come into the Candy Store at night with his Hollywood pals. The actor Donald Sutherland joins the FTA troupe. He's a big name now because he's coming off his breakout role in the Robert Altman hit movie *M*A*S*H*.

If anyone among the brass asks us, we say that *FTA* means "Free the Army." But everyone in the ranks knows the truth. I know it myself from my hitch in West Germany. Whenever you are an enlisted man, the abbreviation *FTA* is always on your lips—if you are not actually coming right out and saying the words. The officers may not know what it means, but the grunts surely do.

You have to understand that it isn't the hippies against the soldiers back then. Thousands of people who are in the military are antiwar. They know better than anyone else that Vietnam is fucked up. There is an antiwar petition, and a thousand sailors on the aircraft carrier *Coral Sea* sign it.

The military freaks out. The brass are terrified about insurrection in the ranks. In the Vietnam war zone, there's a new word—fragging. It's when an enlisted guy tosses a grenade into the tent of a gung-ho officer who is determined to get everyone in his outfit killed. Instead, the officer is the one blown sky-high.

This shit is heavy. This shit is too much. It's the Pentagon's worst nightmare. They want their soldiers dumb and docile, ready to go into battle like sheep to slaughter. They don't want them thinking about it.

And they definitely don't want anyone telling jokes about it. In 1971, we hatch a plan to take the FTA show on the road. We want to go to Vietnam to entertain and enlighten the troops there, but of course the Pentagon prohibits that.

So we chart a two-week tour of the Asian Rim, Hawaii, Okinawa, and the Philippines, winding up in Japan. It's supposed to be me, Peter Boyle, Donald Sutherland, Jane Fonda, and two or three folk singers. Folk singers all around, to the left and right, but mostly to the left. I feel like I am back in Joe and Eddie territory.

Peter Boyle drops out at the last minute. We want to get Faye Dunaway. She's a big star because of *Bonnie and Clyde* and I am absolutely nuts about her. I'm in love with Faye Dunaway. She's right behind Elizabeth Taylor in sexiness.

When Jane Fonda says we have to go to Faye's house and ask her to come on our tour, I freak. "What do I say to her?" I ask Jane. "What can I possibly say to Faye Dunaway?"

"Don't you know?" Jane says. "You say to her the same things you say to me. You say, 'Hi, Faye, I'm Paul.'"

Fonda can see I'm freaking when we walk up to Dunaway's front door. "It'll be okay, Paul," she whispers to me. "Just pretend Faye is nobody. Pretend she's white trash."

Faye Dunaway answers her door and invites us in and says hi all around. "Hi, Faye, I'm Paul," I say. But then she smiles at me and I fall apart. "Jane Fonda tells me you're white trash," I blurt out.

Faye politely declines to go to Asia with us to fuck the military.

We go without her. The whole tour is modeled on Bob Hope's USO shows. He's the USO, we're the UFO—the United Freedom Organization. Nixon's buddy Bob Hope supports the war and entertains the troops. We figure the best way to support the troops is to be against the war that is killing dozens of them every week.

The military hates us. It tries to sabotage our appearances by putting out fake "corrections" listing the wrong time and place. At the back of every audience there are stone-faced military intelligence spooks looking to intimidate the antiwar GIs.

Fonda describes the show as "antiwar vaudeville." We do a lot of fragging-style humor, like a skit where I play a sergeant to Donald Sutherland's officer.

Sutherland: Sergeant, I want to get a watchdog.

Me: But, sir, you're surrounded by thousands of troops. Why would you need a watchdog?

Sutherland: Sergeant, I need a watchdog *because* I'm surrounded by thousands of troops!

On the DC-3 airplane that takes the troupe around Asia, I get up close and personal with Fonda. She has just come off playing a hooker with Donald Sutherland in the movie *Klute,* the role that will win her an Oscar. She's living in Malibu, married to Brigitte Bardot's old husband, the French actor and filmmaker Roger Vadim. A real Hollywood girl.

Jane Fonda as Bree Daniels in *Klute*: "For an hour, I'm the best actress in the world, and the best fuck in the world." And later, when Donald Sutherland turns her down for sex. "Men would pay two hundred dollars for me, and here you are turning down a freebie. You could get a perfectly good dishwasher for that."

Fonda really is lovely in person, fresh-faced and pretty. But I don't buy into her sex-bomb reputation from the movie *Barbarella.* Maybe it's the fact that on the tour she still wears her hair in a Bree Daniels *Klute*-style mullet, which sort of cuts down on her sexiness for me.

The troupe appears outside military bases and we wind up playing to sixty thousand soldiers. They're some of the best audiences I ever have. Those boys are *into* it. Japan especially is a mob scene. Fonda is a big star there because of *Barbarella.* A sobering moment comes when we tour the Hiroshima Peace Memorial Museum. It reminds me what this is all about.

"Foxtrot—Tango—Alpha: FTA Fuck the Army." That's the song with which we open the show. We have a film crew along on the DC-3, and a director named Francine Parker shoots the whole tour. The idea is to make a film of the show that will get FTA much wider exposure than any two-week tour can ever get.

It doesn't work out that way. Fran Parker does cut her film footage together to make a great documentary. It captures not only the act but the bitch sessions we hold for the soldiers, including one I lead for a group of my homeboys from Oakland.

So *F.T.A.*, the documentary, is ready to hit theaters in 1972. It has a distributor, Hollywood mogul Sam Arkoff's American International Pictures. Arkoff normally handles B movies such as *I Was a Teenage Werewolf, The Wasp Woman,* and *A Bucket of Blood.*

But Arkoff is also trying to suck profits out of the social upheavals of the 1960s, like when he puts out the crazed "don't trust anyone over thirty" youth-revolution movie, *Wild in the Streets,* in which Richard has a role.

I'm excited for *F.T.A.*, my first Hollywood screen appearance. It doesn't matter to me that it is a documentary. I am going to be in theaters. On the silver screen, as they say, although to my eyes, screens in movie theaters have always appeared white—in more ways than one.

But in July, without telling anyone in the troupe, Jane Fonda goes to Hanoi. The photograph of her sitting in the seat of a North Vietnamese antiaircraft gun hits the newspapers all over the world. The backlash is brutal.

Richard Nixon has one of his underlings call up Sam Arkoff. You want to put this commie pinko girl in American theaters? Maybe you're some kind of commie pinko yourself? Arkoff, the cowardly film mogul (is there any other kind?), caves. *F.T.A.* is pulled from distribution after a single week.

No one sees my film debut for almost thirty-seven years, when a print of the documentary is discovered. In 2009, *F.T.A.* is broadcast on the Sundance Channel and put out on DVD. As Jane Fonda says, "I wasn't blacklisted—I was gray-listed."

I don't lose sleep over it. I'm too busy losing sleep over another development in my life. I'm up all night keeping Richard Pryor company while he's partying.

He has emerged from his sojourn in the Berkeley wilderness. He's back in Los Angeles, and the two of us begin our dual assault on Fortress Hollywood.

Our first beachhead is a Sunset Strip club that opens in spring 1972, in the same building where Ciro's nightclub used to be, a place that will become my second home, my launching pad, and my battleground.

THE STORE

THE STORE

CHAPTER 16

After being holed up in his little efficiency apartment in Berkeley for a while, listening to Marvin Gaye and reading Malcolm X, Richard ventures out—to find dope connections, among other things. He goes around to clubs like the Purple Onion. He comes back and riffs into a tape recorder about talk he hears on the street.

Before, in Hollywood, I never see Richard read a book, but when I visit him, he's got his nose in *The Autobiography of Malcolm X*, or, more and more, *By Any Means Necessary,* Malcolm's collection of speeches. He's got *The End of White World Supremacy: Four Speeches by Malcolm X* on his shelf, too.

"I like reading him because he shows me that I'm not out of my mind," he tells me. "It's the rest of the world that's nuts, not us."

He jokes when I tell him he's transforming himself. "Yeah," he says, cackling, "I switched from Courvoisier to vodka." As far as I can see, the switch doesn't affect his allegiance to cocaine. He is doing more than ever.

Richard pals around with Claude Brown, author of *Manchild in the Promised Land,* who introduces him to the poet Ishmael Reed and the Berkeley writer Al Young. He's going all intellectual on me.

And all political. I connect him up with my old high school pal Huey P. Newton, now a ferocious Black Panther on the FBI watch list. Huey puts Richard in touch with Angela Davis, another figure who scares the shit out of white America back then.

Richard turns his back on white America. The only white America for him is a line of cocaine. He ventures out to a few small clubs in San Francisco, trying out new routines, developing a whole new voice. He appears at Mandrakes, the hungry i (before it closes in 1970), and Basin Street West.

We cross-pollinate each other. This is the same period I appear at Ye Little Club, trying out routines, developing my whole new voice. It's funny, but running on separate tracks, we both come up with the same thing. We work out a similar way to talk onstage.

It revolves around the word *nigger.*

Richard already uses *nigger* onstage, especially at Maverick's and Redd Foxx's club. But during his exile in Berkeley, he transforms the word into a weapon. *Motherfucker* and *nigger* battle for pride of place in Richard's vocabulary. It's the language of the streets, the words he hears every day around him in Oakland, Berkeley, and San Francisco.

What we both like about the word is that it demonstrates a simple truth. White people cannot say it in front of black people without declaring themselves to be racist.

So when Richard and I use it onstage in front of an audience with both white and black folks in it, we are saying something that white people can't. It's forbidden to them, but allowed to us. Ain't too many things like that. It's liberating.

I study white audiences. Saying "nigger" in public also lets loose a ripple of nervousness, especially in a mixed crowd, which they deal with by laughing.

At Ye Little Club, I open my act a lot of times the same way: "A bunch of niggers in here now." It's like throwing down a gauntlet. Black people laugh out of their recognition of street language, but white folks laugh out of sheer anxiety.

White folks make up the word *nigger,* and then get nervous when I say it. Ain't that a bitch? They shouldn't have made it up! They fucked up. They even made up a song with it. You know the song I'm talking about. "Eeny, meeny, miney, mo . . ."

But they change the words when they see black folks around. "Catch a tiger by the toe . . ."

Tiger? What are they talking about? I'm a ringmaster at the circus, and I know tigers. Tigers don't have toes, as much as claws. There ain't no tigers in America. But there are plenty of niggers in America.

I tell white people that I say "nigger" all the time. I say it a hundred times every morning. It makes my teeth white. I say it, white people think it—what a small white world it is!

Niggerniggerniggernigger . . .

It's a variation on the Lenny Bruce routine I hear in the lesbian bar in North Beach. Use the word enough, and it loses its power to wound.

If President Kennedy got on television and said, "Tonight I'd like to introduce the niggers in my cabinet," and he yelled, "Nigger-nigger-nigger-nigger," at every nigger he saw, until nigger didn't mean anything anymore, until nigger lost its meaning, then maybe you'd never hear a four-year-old come home crying from school 'cause he got called "nigger."

Black folks brandishing *nigger* in public is nothing new. Dick Gregory's autobiography, *Nigger*, gets published in 1964, and he says that every time he hears the word, it's like an advertisment for his book.

I figure it is about time for equal opportunity, since white folks have been spewing "nigger" for centuries. It's always "nigger" this and "nigger" that. I remember that old racist joke, which carries a sad truth. What do you call a black man with a PhD? White folks call him "nigger," of course. I guess Professor Henry Louis Gates, Jr. found that out quick enough up in Cambridge.

Every black person on earth has a story. About the time Richard and I start using it with a vengeance onstage in our routines, Michael Jordan is in school and gets suspended for punching out a white girl who calls him "nigger" on a school bus. Tiger Woods is in kindergarten when some kids tie him up and taunt him with the word. Obama, Oprah, everybody has a "nigger" moment.

It's onstage in Berkeley that I hear the first variation on Richard's most famous riff, the most telling single use of the word *nigger,* I think, in the history of the English language.

White folks get a traffic ticket, they pull their car over and say to the cop, "Gee, officer, what can I do for you? Was I speeding?" Nigger got to be coming at it a whole different way. "I am reaching into my pocket for my license. Because I don't want to be no motherfuckin' accident!"

He's not calling anyone "nigger" here. It's not a slur, it's a description. He's saying the word to describe a class of people in society. The way Richard uses it, *nigger* becomes a means to call out a whole black reality. It's a reality where a simple traffic stop can mean death. And cops stop black folks and treat them like niggers *all the time*. So we know exactly what he is talking about.

Later on, after he puts the routine on his record *That Nigger's Crazy*, Richard reacts with pure delight when he hears that, all over the country, street hustlers and skells are imitating his "I am reaching into my pocket" line verbatim when they get picked up by cops. He is imitating reality, and reality turns around and imitates him. That goes beyond keeping it real—that's keeping it surreal!

While he's still in Berkeley, Richard auditions for Motown's Berry Gordy, Jr., for a role in a movie about Billie Holiday's life. Gordy is just dipping his toe into the film business.

I want to tell Gordy, "No, no, turn back, proud black man! The music business isn't enough bullshit for you? You got to add Hollywood bullshit to your life, too?"

Richard keeps talking about the film project and how it is going to be his big breakthrough. He lets me read the script. Gordy's main Motown diva, Diana Ross, is going to play Lady Day. Richard's part is small and insignificant in the screenplay, which they're calling *Lady Sings the Blues*.

It doesn't matter, since the whole project looks like it's going down the tubes. Paramount, which Gordy is partnering with, pulls out, and Motown has to pay back the $2 million the studio invested. Gordy tells Richard that the project is delayed a year, which I know is Hollywood-speak for "Ain't never gonna happen."

Instead of costarring with a Supreme in a major studio flick, Richard does his own version of my movie *F.T.A.* when he acts in an antiwar sketch comedy called *Dynamite Chicken*. Just like Jane Fonda and Donald Sutherland are behind

F.T.A., John Lennon and Yoko Ono are behind Richard's film. They get a whole bunch of celebrities to appear, people like Lenny Bruce, Jimi Hendrix, B. B. King, and Yoko herself.

Funnily enough—seeing as how *Dynamite Chicken* is an antimilitary movie—the movie tanks. Richard throws himself into his three major consolations—vodka, cocaine, and pussy.

"I'm doing so much shit, the drug dealers are embarrassed for me," he says when I visit him in Berkeley. "They look at me with pity in their eyes."

"Not enough pity for them to stop selling to you," I say.

"Not enough pity in the world for that," he says, cackling.

I've seen a lot of pussy hounds, but never one like Richard. He rips through women faster than a rock star. He gets after my cousin Alice. He goes to bed with Diane DeMarko.

"You know, he's got a big one," she tells me afterward. She holds her hands out about a foot apart.

"No, I wouldn't know," I say. "We're close, but we ain't that close."

Richard reminds me of a frantic kid, running around trying to distract himself. He discovers Asian food and is always dragging me down to San Francisco's Chinatown. He buys a samurai sword and starts watching kung fu movies obsessively. He wants to make a kung fu movie himself. He wants to write. He wants to act.

I can tell Berkeley is over for him. It's done the trick. Richard's energized again. If he keeps up with this frantic bullshit, he's going to explode. I keep suggesting that stand-up is where it's at, the only place a black man can speak his mind without Hollywood going all Frankenstein on him.

I hear about a new place on the Strip in L.A., just opened by a couple of old-school schtick comics named Sammy

Shore and Rudy De Luca. I tell Richard it's time for him to come back to Los Angeles. His exile in Berkeley has gone on long enough.

"Come down and do some shows at Sammy Shore's new club," I say.

Richard is slated to go to the Apollo in Harlem to debut his new act. He needs a small club to try out material. But Ye Little Club is too little for him.

"What's the place called?" he asks.

"They're naming it the Store," I say.

"Just like the Candy Store," Richard says.

"You got to watch yourself there," I say. "Folks are telling me white comics listen to your act, steal your best lines, and open in Vegas with the shit they steal."

"Ain't nobody going to steal nothing off me," Richard says. "Motherfucker wouldn't know what to do with it."

He is right. Richard is never worried about anyone raiding his material. It's too much his. His delivery puts a stamp on it. Some other comic could do a Richard Pryor routine word for word, and it wouldn't come out as funny.

He closes down the dumpy Berkeley apartment, emerges from exile, and in spring 1972, we show up at the new club.

CHAPTER 17

For the next ten years, all through the stand-up boom of the 1970s, the Comedy Store on Sunset becomes my main base of operations.

Sammy Shore, a geeky-looking old-style comedian with curly hair and a fleshy nose, opens the club. It's his spot, but he's never there. He's always on the road. He's a warm-up comic, the guy who comes on before the big act and gets the audience going. His main gig is opening for Elvis in Vegas. He likes to call himself the Man Who Makes Elvis Laugh.

In Sammy's absence, his wife, Mitzi, works the door. When it opens, the club isn't even a room. It's a bin. Just a space hollowed out of the huge Ciro's building. There are no amenities, no decorations.

But it's not tucked away in Beverly Hills like Ye Little Club, it's right there on the dogleg of the Strip, between the Whisky and all the other rock clubs to the west and the Chateau Marmont to the east.

Mitzi is a good businesswoman. She keeps enlarging the club. The first space is known as the Original Room, and when she takes over the whole building, she opens the Main Room. Then she makes room for a small space, originally designated for female comics, and calls it the Belly Room.

Gradually, during the course of May 1972, Mitzi warms the place up. She hangs ferns. She puts a painting behind the bar. The decorative style goes from meat-packing warehouse to 1970s nightclub. A sign on the wall reads THE JOKES ARE FREE, THE DRINKS ARE 75 CENTS.

Minding the Store: Robin Williams, Mitzi Shore, and me at the Comedy Store

Sammy Shore going on the road is the best thing that ever happens to comedy in L.A. If the Comedy Store were left up to him, I'm sure it would go out of business. He is a gag man, not a businessman. His wife is the powerhouse. She is always there, at her post at the cash register, playing mother hen to the comics. The lady knows what she's doing.

"I do it all for the comics," she says, and a lot of the performers who show up are emotionally needy and love her mothering.

One small example: Mitzi gives away cigarettes to nervous comedians. It's a brilliant ministrategy for running a comedy club. Stand-ups love them some cigarettes. Most of them smoke like the goal of their life is to get lung cancer. Mitzi hands out bubble gum, too, and if comics are really nervous, they take both. The devil is in the details.

Sammy Shore comes back to his own club after being on the road for a month. He doesn't recognize the place. He tells his wife he wants to do a show.

"I'll see if I can fit you in tomorrow night," Mitzi says.

Sammy sees which way the wind is blowing, both in his club and in the marriage. He and Mitzi divorce by the time the year is out. In the settlement, Mitzi gets the club.

She's got the club, but she still needs the laughs. If there's one performance that makes the Store a success, it's in June 1972, when Richard decides to try out new material two months after the club opens.

He begins his act by giving notice that things have changed with him. He's a new comic. He goes straight for the white people in the audience:

I notice on the nights in the clubs here, like, white people come out early on Saturday night, and go home, and leave it to the niggers. It's great to think that we can all sit in the same club together, white and black, and not understand each other. It's amazing, it can only happen in America.

Once he gets rolling, it's the new Richard, born in Berkeley, midwifed by Malcolm X and Marvin Gaye.

I used to be running from the cops and shit, 'cause we had a curfew. Niggers had to be home by eleven, Negroes by twelve. White cops worked at night, and if they caught you, your ass would be in trouble. "Get your hands up, black boy!" "I didn't do nothing!" "Shut up and get your hands up against the wall." "There ain't no wall." "Find one." But I used to love getting arrested in Peoria on Saturday night because if you got in the lineup, that was like being in show business. 'Cause, like, all the ugly white girls who couldn't get any, say niggers raped them.

All the copycat Cosby bullshit burns off Richard while he is in Berkeley. It's like he's firing up some base. He gets rid of all the impurities. This is the pure shit.

Richard has already put some of these routines on record, his second album, *Craps (After Hours)*. It is mostly recorded at Red Foxx's and other South Central black clubs. You can pick out my laugh on the tracks, booming out, backing Richard up. This shit is funny.

With Richard's appearance, the Store turns a corner. It becomes a hip club for celebrities. Richard is a stand-up comic who wants to be a movie star, but in the Store I see movie star after movie star wishing they were comedians, long before there is any actor-turned-rapper or rapper-turned-actor or child-star-turned-tramp or tramp-turned-child-star. Comics are sexy, comics are the rage. And the Store is our lair.

Film, TV, and music stars turn up at the Store all the time, people such as Goldie Hawn, Burt Reynolds, Sally Field, Donny Osmond, the Captain & Tenille, and Lee Majors, from the *Six Million Dollar Man,* comes in with his girlfriend, Farrah Fawcett.

Farrah and I recognize each other from an encounter at a traffic light on Sunset a few years before. I am always seeing celebrities in their cars in L.A. I get the strangest stare from Michael Jackson on Hollywood Boulevard. It's like he's trying to run a Vulcan mind meld on my ass.

This time, I tap my horn as I pull up alongside another convertible at a stoplight on Sunset. A pretty girl with windblown honey-colored hair is in the car next to mine, sitting in the driver's seat as though it were a throne at a beauty pageant. This is a year before she becomes well known.

The two of us, both cars with their tops down, alone at the red. That's enough of an introduction in Hollywood.

"Hey," I say.

"Hi," Farrah says.

"Are you an actress?"

"Yeah."

"Done anything?"

"Not yet." She smiles. Megawatt teeth.

"Whoa!" I pull down my sun visor and shade my eyes as a joke. She laughs.

"Hollywood is going to eat you alive," I say. "This town is going to *eat you alive, girl!"*

She laughs again. "I hope so," she says.

"What's your name?"

"Farrah Fawcett."

Using my Miss Amerae powers, I make the light turn green. I greenlight Farrah Fawcett. Lovingly, with the deepest of regrets, we pull away and go our separate ways.

Next time I see her it's on TV. The bad guy points a gun at her and she kicks it out of his hand. The next time I see her after that, she's in the audience at the Store, sitting next to Lee Majors and laughing at my routine.

When Richard leaves the Comedy Store after his act, going off in search of drugs, I stay behind and play Whack-A-Mole on white people. I usually make sure I go on after midnight, since that's when the black folks come out, like they're vampires.

My audience. Black people and brave white people.

You know, white people are sensitive. They're like little white rabbits. They'll leave. They'll get the fuck out of a place. "Let's go, let's go, let's go." Then you got them ballsy white people. "This nigger doesn't intimidate me. I'll stay till the sun rises! We'll see if this is a nigger vampire!"

The Comedy Store still doesn't know what kind of club it is. There are all these hungry young comics like me and Richard, plus a lot of the New York guys like Jimmie Walker, Freddie Prinze, Gabe Kaplan, and Steve Landesberg. They're transplants. New York used to be the capital of comedy. Now it's L.A.

Then there are all these older professionals, guys who came up in the Borscht Belt and have been doing their schticks for years. They can't figure out young audiences and they're so tour addled that half the time they don't know what the hell city they're in. They just trot out the same setups and punch lines. They all want to be in Vegas.

Mitzi is all about mentoring us young comics and easing the old guys out. For one thing, she knows the young ones are less likely to complain about not getting paid. None of us are paid during our first years at the Store. We work for free, for bubble gum and cigarettes.

Mitzi has it in her mind that we are "workshopping" our acts. The payoff will come some other time, from someone else, from TV, somewhere, anywhere, as long as it's not from her.

For a few people, it works out. All the New York comics get TV shows. Jimmie Walker does *Good Times,* with everybody in the country saying his signature line, "Dy-no-mite!"

Freddie Prinze, who is going out with Lenny Bruce's daughter, Kitty, nails the lead role on *Chico and the Man.* Gabe Kaplan goes on *Welcome Back, Kotter.* Steve Landesberg (who comes up with one of my favorite lines, "Honesty is the best policy, but insanity is a better defense"), gets a part on *Barney Miller.*

All the time I'm thinking, *My turn next!* If I were a Borscht Belt comic, I'd be asking, "What am I, chopped liver?" I don't sit around waiting. I am always working either at Ye Little Club or the Store. But the phone never rings with my big TV break.

I know that producers who pass me by are leaving millions of dollars on the table. They say the profit motive is sacred, but it's not true. Racism trumps capitalism. Hollywood prefers to pass up a program that I know I can make a hit, rather than work with a proud black man like me. I make them too nervous. I freak them out. It reminds me of my guerrilla newspaper in high school, or my alternative talent show. You don't want to work with me? Fine. I'll do it myself.

I'm surprised by the ignorance of the people around me at the Store, including all the young white comedians I'm hanging with. It's like for them, the world began yesterday, and it starts and stops in the white neighborhoods of Brooklyn.

I'm reading a lot of African history, black history, all kinds of history, so I start working it into my act.

Don't let Chinese people fool you—they didn't invent rice. Rice didn't come from China, it came from Africa, like a lot of shit, we invented a lot of shit, okay? The piano. The English found the piano in the middle of the jungle and brought it back to England. They put white keys on it, fucked it up, ruined it. So Uncle Ben's black ass belongs on the rice box, because we introduced rice to Chinese people. We scared 'em—we threw the rice at 'em. They said, "Don't touch it, pick it up with sticks!" The rest is history.

I sort of mildly wonder if it's this kind of material that's closing doors in my face in Hollywood. It ain't that I think of changing or making it more pale to suit the tastes of the Hollywood suits. I'm just curious, that's all. My act doesn't strike me or Richard as radical. Neither of us can understand how anyone can really be offended by it. It's the truth.

"Nixon in China, now that shit is offensive," Richard says. "What you do, Mr. Mooney, that's just keeping it real. You ain't offensive. You're colorful."

Richard has a love-hate thing with Hollywood. I just settle on hating it. But he can't give up his fantasy of becoming a movie star.

The month after the Comedy Store opens, Johnny Carson moves *The Tonight Show* from New York City to Los Angeles—actually, to Burbank. Johnny will have Richard on, because he's too popular to ignore, but his producer Fred De Cordova blocks my shit. Freddie doesn't want to know me. He hires everyone else in the world, not me. I think he'd have a fucking statue on the show before he'd call me.

I watch comic after young comic, the same ones I started with at the Comedy Store, I see them all flap away on wings of money, flying off to TVland. Not me.

Richard and I realize something. If we are going to crack television, we are going to have to do it ourselves.

CHAPTER 18

Along with the Store opening and Johnny Carson moving his show to California, another thing happens at the beginning of 1972. Redd Foxx gets his own sitcom.

Ever since Richard appears at his club, Redd is our main man. Richard rents one of Redd's houses. We see his act at least once a week. He's a lot like his character Fred G. Sanford. He doesn't suffer fools. For a long time, he's too pissed off at the American government to pay income taxes.

Norman Lear, the producer of the Archie Bunker hit *All in the Family*, sees Redd in the movie *Cotton Comes to Harlem*, an action comedy based on a crime novel by the great Chester Himes. Himes is one of my all-time favorite writers. He leads a hard-knock life, including a stretch in an Ohio prison, but he always says he never encounters the real depth of racism and gets "saturated with hate" until he comes to Los Angeles.

In the 1940s, Warner Bros. briefly hires Himes as a screenwriter, but then studio head Jack Warner hears about it; "I don't want no goddamned niggers on this lot." Himes turns his back on America and lives in Europe for the rest of his life.

In the late 1960s, Hollywood still has a segregated frame of mind. *Cotton Comes to Harlem* is one of the few films that the studios allow a black man to make—the actor Ossie Davis is the director—and it's a hit.

Redd plays a character named Uncle Bud in *Cotton,* and steals every scene he's in. Based on that performance, Norman Lear proposes to Redd that he take the lead role in a new TV show Lear and his producing partner Bud Yorkin are developing about a junkman and his son in Watts.

Like *All in the Family,* the sitcom is based on a hit British TV show. *Sanford and Son* is a remake of a popular BBC program called *Steptoe and Son.*

Redd knows he wants black writers on staff, because *Sanford and Son* is going to be a black show—the first American television sitcom with a primarily black cast since *Amos 'n' Andy* gets cancelled. Naturally, Redd suggests to Richard and me that we write for his new show. Miracle of miracles, the producers hire us.

It doesn't come that easy. Richard and I have to jump through all sorts of Hollywood hoops to get taken on as writers. It ain't Lear or Yorkin, they're all for us. It's the system.

You'd think that with the star of the show behind you, it'd be a slam dunk. You'd think that a monster hit like *All in the Family* gives the producers a little juice, that they can hire whoever they want.

But racism trumps capitalism. The NBC brass hem and haw like mules. They want their own people as writers. Their own white people. The kind with the complexion for the protection.

"We're having trouble finding black comedy writers," the NBC people would say in meetings, right to our black faces.

Baffled and apparently invisible to them, I reply, "I guess if I'm running this show, I would have trouble finding white ones."

Richard and I are tossed a couple of bones. We get our Writers Guild cards for doing two *Sanford* episodes in the second season, "The Dowry" and "Sanford and Son and Sister Makes Three." Redd fights and brings me back for one more episode in season three, "Fred Sanford, Legal Eagle."

The kind of material I write is maybe the reason I'm on the Hollywood blacklist. This is from the "Legal Eagle" episode, where Demond Wilson as Lamont Sanford is all pissed off for getting a traffic ticket he didn't deserve.

> *Fred Sanford to Lamont:* If you had the green light, you can't get a ticket.
> *Lamont:* You can if the light is green and you're black and the cop is white.
> *Fred:* You got to fight it.
> *Lamont:* Don't be ridiculous. You can't fight a traffic ticket.
> *Fred:* I'm not ridiculous, you are. You get a ticket from a white cop in a blue uniform in a black neighborhood. It makes you so mad that you're seeing red. But you ain't going to fight it because you're too yellow. Now what are you? A man or a box of crayons?

Redd as Fred loves it. But it's the kind of material that cuts close to the bone. And it gets me no favors with the NBC brass.

They always say it's too "angry" when they want to block you. But I'm not angry. I'm the happiest man I know. I just dedicate myself to keeping it real. So I never get invited back to write for *Sanford and Son.*

The "Legal Eagle" episode is still being censored today. My writing still pushes buttons. This is the scene in the original version where Fred confronts the white cop who writes Lamont the traffic ticket.

> *Fred*: Hey, look here, why don't you arrest some white drivers?
> *White cop*: I do.
> *Fred [gesturing around to all the black people in the docket]:* Well, where are they? Look at all these niggers in here!

The studio audience goes nuts. They absolutely go crazy with laughter and clapping and hollering. They are all from Los Angeles, and they know the "driving while black" policies of the LAPD all too well. Redd has to wait for the laughter and applause to die down before he unleashes my tail-end zinger.

> *Fred:* There's enough niggers in here to make a Tarzan movie!

On the DVD they're selling of *Sanford and Son* nowadays, there's none of that shit. They cut the whole scene. They wreck the flow of the show. The action suddenly jumps like a train off the tracks. If you don't know the original, you can't figure out what's up.

Eventually, Redd gets fed up with the Hollywood bullshit, too. *Sanford and Son* is a hit show, top ten every season it's on, peaking at number two behind Archie Bunker. Plus it's aired in the so-called death slot of Friday evening, when no show ever succeeds, and it still kills. But it strikes Redd that he's not getting the props someone in his position should.

"I get tired of their bullshit," Redd tells me and Richard. "Man, I'm too black for Hollywood."

It's the first time I hear the phrase. But Richard and I recognize what he's talking about. Los Angeles is a racist place. I think about Lead Belly: "Yeah, it's a bourgeois town."

Redd demands that NBC hire more black writers. The network drags its feet and does nothing. Redd tells them again and again that the white writers they hire don't understand the black experience. NBC ignores him.

So Redd quits. Here's NBC blowing a top-ten show, killing the goose that is laying golden eggs. They'd rather do that, losing out on millions of dollars for their stockholders, than let a black man tell them what to do.

Racism trumps capitalism.

Right around this time, Richard also gets disgusted with the whole film-studio establishment. His dream of being a movie star isn't panning out. He decides to take his act on the road. After trying out his material at the Store, he opens at the Apollo and plays the whole country for black folks in Chicago, Detroit, and Kansas City.

It's like stand-up is his safety net. He can always make $50,000, $100,000, or even $300,000 a year onstage, enough to support his alimonies and his habits. There's a whole audience out there that the white entertainment industry is ignoring. And those are the people Richard seeks out.

When Richard does finally get a break from butting his head up against the wall of Fortress Hollywood, naturally it's courtesy of a black entrepreneur. Berry Gordy doesn't let the movie *Lady Sings the Blues* die after all. Paramount pulling out its $2 million can't stop him. He puts his own $2 million into the movie and lets the cameras roll.

It could have been a recipe for a disaster: a rookie movie producer puts his favorite diva in a starring role. Instead,

Berry Gordy shows Hollywood how it's done. He makes a good movie. Gordy's first production knocks down a bunch of Oscar nominations. I watch that shit today, *Lady* still holds up. Diana Ross wins a Golden Globe for her first film performance, but loses out on the Oscar to Liza Minnelli in *Cabaret*.

Richard knocks me out with what he does with the tragic, nameless character of the "Piano Man." What's on the page in the script is light-years away from what's onscreen. Richard riffs and improvises like a crazy man. The scene where Billie hears of the death of her mother is only a couple of bland lines in the script. Richard's reaction is all him.

He's so good that, watching him, I forget he's my best friend. I even forget he's Richard. I'm sucked into believing the character like everyone else does. But I also see the real Richard in it loud and clear all the way through. In the "that's me at the door" party scene, I recognize good-times Richard. Night after night, party after party, I watch him get down exactly like that.

The Piano Man character is sort of loosely based on Billie Holiday's real accompanist, Bobby Tucker. "Mr. B" is legendary, and works with everybody from the other "Mr. B," Billy Eckstein, to Johnny Hartman. He is forgotten now. When he dies in 2007, he doesn't even warrant an obit. Just another black genius gone.

Richard makes Piano Man totally his own. He's convinced that the role will be his big break. He's going to be a star. Producers are going to come knocking on his door. We both think he's going to get nominated for an Academy Award.

It doesn't happen. Producers only offer him jack-shit film roles to follow up *Lady*. This is the business Richard wants to succeed in more than any other, and he keeps hitting brick walls.

He does earn himself a few perks. The Daisy is a private club just like the Candy Store, but more racist. The hostess at the place always treats us like we have leprosy. She lets us in, but looks stony-faced and unfriendly. We call her the Dry-Ice Queen, because she is colder than ice.

Then she hears Richard has a role in *Lady Sings the Blues*. She gets all gushy over us. "Oh, you're the black Paul Newman," she coos to me, while rubbing herself against Richard's body like a cat after milk.

I remember Marilyn Monroe's bitter comment about Hollywood: "It's a place where they'll pay you a thousand dollars for a kiss and fifteen cents for your soul." Richard wasn't getting what he wanted from producers during this period, but he got a lot of love from women, which was almost as important to him.

CHAPTER 19

Richard and I knock around Hollywood. He is a lot better off than I am. He is steps ahead of me in the biz. He's got TV. He's got albums. He's done movies. Plus there's the little fact that he's a genius. I'm just pretty. But Hollywood chews up and spits out genius and prettiness.

As writers, we're the lowest men on the film-business totem pole. (We hear a joke about a girl, the dumbest-ass bitch in the world, she wants to break into movies. She goes to Hollywood and fucks the screenwriter.) Producers will always kill you with praise before delivering their favorite line: "Your script is perfect—let me tell you how to change it." Hollywood producers have fucked up more movies than they've ever gotten made. They ruin scripts that would have been classics. They're like ass backward Rumpelstiltskins. They spin gold into straw.

Around this time, I get my first agent, Al Winkur. The man with the golden tongue. He can talk his way into hell and back out again. He opens every door for me. Problem is, Al's checkbook isn't as golden as his tongue. He tends to write checks that bounce.

My natural element:
Onstage, the place where
I feel most alive

"You can take all the sincerity in Hollywood," says the old-school comedian Fred Allen, "put it in a flea's navel, and still have room left for three caraway seeds and an agent's heart."

That isn't Al Winkur. He has a huge heart. He has the best intentions. He wants me to work. But he is up against Fortress Hollywood, and twenty-five years after they chase Chester Himes out of town, they still have problems with "goddamned niggers on the lot."

I work almost every night, at either the Store or Ye Little Club, but that doesn't put food on the table. So I work strip clubs. All the old-fashioned burlesque shows, the ones that put comics on between the strippers, are dying out, but there are a few left, tucked away on side streets off Sunset. If you're lucky at one of these clubs, the management pays you $50 for a night's work, a dozen short sets. But I'll take it.

In November 1973, Richard gets a gig on Lily Tomlin's TV special that wins him an Emmy. Tomlin first comes to Hollywood for the hit 1960s sketch show *Laugh-In*. She loves Richard and hires him as a writer and performer for her program, *Lily*.

It's the first time Richard works with Lorne Michaels, who takes a producing and writing credit on the program. Working with Tomlin on her special and with Flip Wilson on his show means Richard's back on national TV, after being absent since his Sullivan days.

Richard is jazzed. It's really happening for him. But Hollywood has a way of setting you up just to knock you down. I'm always surprised at Richard's forbearance. Producers treat him like dog shit over and over, and he just goes back for more.

I'm a bystander when Richard gets a Hollywood project that once again breaks his heart. In fact, *Blazing Saddles* almost kills him. The producer Mel Brooks sells an idea to Warner Bros. about a black cowboy. He wants the script process to be like his old days as a writer for the 1950s Sid Caesar hit *Your Show of Shows*: a bunch of comics in a room workshopping the screenplay. Mel Brooks knows his comedy. He's smart enough to know who is the funniest man on the planet. He hires Richard.

I read the treatment that Brooks sells to Warner. It's called *Tex X*. There are no laughs in it. It's not even clever.

"You sure you want to do this, man?" I ask Richard.

"Don't worry," he says. "I can make it funny. They're going to hire me to play Black Bart. It's the lead!"

Richard throws his heart and soul into it. I've never seen him more focused. He goes off every day, on time, and works in Brooks's office. Mel's got two other writers, Norman Steinberg and Alan Uger, who did work on the TV show *The Corner Bar.*

But Richard is the king shit in that group. They change the title of the movie to *Black Bart,* then to *Blazing Saddles.* Richard writes killer dialog.

Bart: Mornin', ma'am. And isn't it a lovely mornin'?
Old woman: Up yours, nigger.

He comes up with the scene where Black Bart takes himself hostage.

Bart [*pointing his own gun to his head*]: Hold it! Next man makes a move, the nigger gets it!
Olson: Hold it, men. He's not bluffing.
Doctor: Listen to him, men. He's just crazy enough to do it!
Bart: Drop it! Or I swear I'll blow this nigger's head all over this town! [*in a prissy* Gone with the Wind *accent*] Oh, lordy, lord, he's des'prit! Do what he say, do what he say!

And he writes the most memorable scene in the movie, where the cowboys sit around the fire, cutting farts.

This last one is too much for Warner Bros. It's the funniest scene in the movie, the one everyone remembers, and Warner Bros. insists that Brooks change it. Mel insists the scene stays as written.

He wins that battle, but loses the war. Warner Bros. won't let him hire Richard for the lead. This is a character the man created, and the studio refuses to let him play it.

The suits don't like Richard. He's got a reputation as unreliable, for being a doper and a drinker. But that's just their excuse. The real reason they don't like him is because he makes them uneasy.

Who do they hire instead? Cleavon Little. He's another actor from *Cotton Comes to Harlem*. Richard knows him. They work together on a *Mod Squad* episode, "The Connection." Cleavon is a good Negro, clean-cut and articulate. Above all, he's *safe*.

I'll give you a dollar if you can name another Cleavon Little picture off the top of your head. His career goes nowhere after *Blazing Saddles*. He finishes up as a TV actor. He's fine, he's okay, but he's not a genius.

On the other hand, can you picture *Blazing Saddles* with Richard Pryor as the lead? Ridiculous, right? It'd be the bomb. It'd rank as the funniest comedy of all time. Richard could do something with Black Bart that Cleavon Little could never do. He could make the character dangerous as well as hilarious.

Maybe that's the real reason why Warner Bros. denies Richard the part. The studio brass are threatened by him. White folks are always threatened by black men who don't bow and scrape in front of them. Once again, racism trumps capitalism. Warner Bros. misses out on millions of dollars in stockholder profits because the executives are ruled by their prejudices instead of their brains. Serves them right.

Losing the role cuts Richard off at the knees. I see him go through all the stages of grief. He denies the fact that he's not getting Black Bart, he rages, he bargains, he gets depressed. "Fuck Hollywood" becomes his mantra. Richard chills his friendship with Cleavon Little and bad-mouths Mel Brooks for promising him the part to begin with. He's devastated and thoroughly disgusted. He wins a Writers Guild of America Award for the *Blazing Saddles* screenplay, but that's just like rubbing salt on his wound. It takes him a full two years to get over his disappointment.

Once again, stand-up saves him.

"You better get back onstage," I tell him.

"Fuck Hollywood," he says. His automatic answer to everything.

"All right, you don't have to work in L.A. Go back to Berkeley again, do a show up there," I say. "Do something, man, don't just sit around and mope."

"Fuck you, too," Richard says. He's stuffing his face with the gross national product of Bolivia. Cocaine is like the full moon for Richard. It brings out his werewolf.

And a werewolf always attacks those nearest to him first. When the dope and alcohol crank up, I know enough to leave. I see a pentagram glowing on Richard's forehead, and that's my cue to bolt.

But he takes my advice. We go up to San Francisco, and he records a show in front of one of Don Cornelius's *Soul Train* audiences. He does a riff about a wino confronting Dracula:

Where you from, fool? Transylvania? I know where it is, nigger! You ain't the smartest motherfucker in the world, you know. Even though you is the ugliest. Oh, yeah, you an ugly motherfucker. Why don't you get your teeth fixed, nigger? That shit hanging all out of your mouth. Why don't you go to an orthodontist? That's a dentist, you know.

I know what this riff is all about. It's Richard talking back to Hollywood. The street-smart folk wisdom of the wino, confronting the white world, confronting film executives. The whole bloodsucking bunch of them. He's showing how much smarter he is than they are. He's showing that he's not afraid of them. Wino on Dracula, black on white, ghetto street on executive suite.

Richard decides to name the album after a phrase we say all the time: "That nigger's crazy!" When some fool is kung fu dancing on the floor at Maverick's, we cackle to each other and say, "That nigger's crazy!" We say it about Redd Foxx, about Flip Wilson and Billy Dee Williams and Marlon Brando, about anybody we damn well please.

Richard takes the phrase and applies it to himself. His album *That Nigger's Crazy* blows up huge. It's everywhere. In South Central, in Inglewood and Compton, we hear it coming out of house stereos as we drive by. People put it on tape and listen in their cars and boom boxes. And it ain't just black folks. It's a massive crossover hit.

Richard's record company, Stax, goes out of business just as *That Nigger's Crazy* is released; people can't even buy it, and the album still blows up huge. Richard just switches labels and brings it out on Reprise. He makes so much money that he can finally afford his coke habit.

He's a superstar. But he's not totally happy, because what he really wants is to make it as a movie star. He's broken out, though, and *That Nigger's Crazy* wins him a Grammy for Best Comedy Album.

For all Richard's success, I never feel a shred of envy or anything like that. Something in my character doesn't allow me to be jealous of anybody else. It's Mama's gift again. I have too much fun being me. And I have fun stepping on the Celebrity Express with Richard.

It's wild. I have the best of both worlds. I get to go to clubs and concerts and parties with Richard, but I don't have to feel all the stresses and strains that make him Hoover up lines of coke and suck down fifths of Smirnoff every single waking second.

Plus we always crack each other up. No matter how strung out or high or fucked up or sick Richard gets, he never loses his sense of humor. I have never encountered anyone like him. He can be raging, screaming at this or that woman, or this or that Hollywood executive, and if I drop a line that tickles him, he turns on a dime. That laugh redeems all.

I go with him to Las Vegas, and they give us a huge suite. It's like a castle. I go in, and as we head to our bedrooms, I say in a heavy German accent, "Good night, Dr. Franken-stein!" Richard cracks up. Our favorite riff.

Clubs and concerts and parties and casinos—and yachts. This is the period when we find ourselves on a yacht Richard rented, anchored out in Santa Monica Bay. Way off to the east are the lights of Los Angeles. The barking of the seals on the Channel Islands sounds across the water. And there's a clutch of pretty people on the boat.

One of the pretty people is a very pretty twenty-three-year-old girl who sits on Richard's lap. In her bikini, her breasts look like two puppies trying to crawl out from behind a pair of eighteen-cent postage stamps. Richard is the cat with nine lives. He was born lucky, with a horseshoe stuck up his ass.

Earlier that evening, Richard opens the yacht's safe to show us the million dollars in cash that he keeps there. Just a little sailing-around money in his yacht safe.

We sit around on deck and listen to the seals. "What are you thinking, Mr. Mooney?" Richard asks me.

"What are *you* thinking?" I say back to him.

"I'm thinking this young girl here is going to fuck me to death," he says.

I say, "Well, I'm thinking about how I can get that million dollars that's in the safe, sink this boat with all you on it, and get away—and goddamn if I can swim."

Richard laughs so hard he dumps the puppy girl off his lap. We just look at each other and howl. We done stepped into some deep, deep shit.

Life is beautiful.

CHAPTER 20

Lorne Michaels wants Richard Pryor. Needs him. Has to have him. Richard Pryor wants Paul Mooney. Without Paul Mooney, Lorne Michaels can't have Richard Pryor.

Lorne Michaels is the executive producer of *Saturday Night Live*. NBC's late-night ensemble sketch show is in its first season, back when it's called just *Saturday Night,* because sportscaster Howard Cosell already has a show named *Saturday Night Live.*

Lorne's show hasn't broken out yet. No one's watching. Nobody knows who the fuck John Belushi is, or Chevy Chase, Gilda Radner, Dan Aykroyd, or any of the other cast members.

Because he worked with Richard on the Lily Tomlin special, Lorne knows that the surest way to light a fire under his ratings is to get Richard to guest-host. Richard is hotter than a pistol. *That Nigger's Crazy* is taking over the world.

Richard plays hard to get. He doesn't much like Lorne Michaels. He lays down conditions: I want to bring in my own writers. I want to bring in Shelley, my ex-wife, to do a cameo. I want this. I want that. Lorne keeps saying "okay," but then he doesn't do anything. So Richard blows him off.

Richard's on tour, playing a jai alai arena in Miami, when Lorne and his NBC execs fly down to woo him. Richard tells them he wants black writers on the show.

"I don't want white people putting words into my mouth," he says. "I don't get Paul, you don't get me."

Lorne flies me out to meet with them all in Miami. I go into the green room at the jai alai arena and they are all sitting there, Lorne Michaels and his NBC suits. They cross-examine me.

How long have you been writing?

Since your mama aborted you, motherfucker.

How long have you been doing comedy?

Since your daddy sold your mama's pussy on the street corner, bitch.

All right, so I don't say anything that balls-out nasty. But I am pissed. What is this? It is like I am in Mississippi, with a bright light shining in my face, having to pass a literacy test to be able to vote. "Fuck you and everybody who looks like you," I want to say.

The NBC execs are not used to dealing with black writers—not black writers with power, black writers with leverage over them. They dither. They ask me more questions. They smile and smile. But I see the horns and forked tongues that Richard always sees.

I think about all my nights at the Store and Ye Little Club, I think about Maverick's Flat and Redd Foxx's, I think about the circus and Joe and Eddie and *Dance Party* and *Sanford and Son* and all my other gigs stretching back to infinity. I've paid my dues. Have you, motherfuckers?

But I am calm. I know that Lorne doesn't have any choice. He wants his show to succeed. He wants the hottest comic in the country to appear on *Saturday Night*. George Carlin didn't do it for him, or Paul Simon, Robert Klein, Lily Tomlin, or any of the other people he's had in to guest-host.

Lorne has to have Richard. I go into these ridiculous meetings knowing I'm going to get hired. We're in New York at the NBC Studios in Rockefeller Center a month later.

After all the posturing with the suits—like some cons facing off in the yard of San Quentin or something—Richard and I fit right in with the *Saturday Night Live* crew. Richard immediately strikes up a friendship with John Belushi. They bond as drug buddies.

The set is nothing but a crackhouse. Weed and heroin and pills. Plus plenty of Richard's favorite, cocaine.

The other writers start off by calling Richard "Dick Pryor." I know Richard. "Dick" reminds him of the early days, when nobody respected him. I know that I can call him that (though I almost never do), maybe Jim Brown and a few other people can call him that, but out of anyone else's mouth it feels like they're talking down to him. He sets them straight. I guess this scares Michael O'Donoghue, the show's head writer. We don't see him again for the whole week.

Garrett Morris, the token Negro in the ensemble, isn't in any of the sketches we work on. I think, *Why not? Is there a quota in place?* Richard and I both secretly regard Morris as a perfect Negro, specializing in clownish comedy. He doesn't seem to be a part of the ensemble, like he's some separate but equal cast member.

When Richard hears NBC has put a seven-second delay in place for just this show, he blows up. None of the other hosts get this restriction, just Richard. It's crap. It's demeaning. But it's in their nature. Anything the white man can do to control a black man, they will do.

During rehearsals—whenever he manages to show up at them and is not boycotting the show in a funk—Richard unleashes a string of "motherfucker's" and "nigger's" in his act. Lorne freaks out. The other members of the cast are mostly too stoned to follow the battles being waged right underneath their coke-encrusted noses.

Except for Chevy Chase. He keeps sending emissaries to me, script assistants and staff writers. They ask meekly, "Could you please write something for Chevy and Richard?" He arranges for Lorne to sit down with me and plead his case. Toward the end of the week, as the Saturday show time approaches, he starts following me around himself, like a lamb after Bo Peep.

"Richard hates me, doesn't he?" Chevy asks me.

"He doesn't hate you," I say, even though I know Richard does indeed despise Chevy.

Chevy's not convinced. He goes off muttering to himself. "Richard hates me, Richard hates me, Richard hates me." Like it's his mantra or something.

Soon enough he's back tugging on my sleeve. "Write something for us, will you?" he pleads. "I have to get some air time with Richard."

Finally, in the early afternoon on Thursday, I hand Lorne a sheet of paper.

"What's this?"

"You've all been asking me to put Chevy and Richard together," I say.

After all the bullshit I've been put through to get here, the fucking cross-examination Lorne subjects me to, I decide to do a job interview of my own.

Chevy's the boss, interviewing Richard for a janitor's job. The white personnel interviewer suggests they do some word association, so he can test if the black man's fit to employ. He kicks it off:

Chevy Chase: White.
   Richard: Black.
Chase: Bean.
   Richard: Pod.
Chase: Negro.
   Richard: Whitey.
Chase: Tar baby.
   Richard [miffed]: What did you say?
Chase: Tar baby.
   Richard: Ofay.
Chase: Colored.
   Richard [bringing it]: Redneck!
Chase: Jungle bunny!
   Richard: Peckerwood!
Chase: Burrhead!
   Richard: Cracker.
Chase: Spearchucker.
   Richard: White trash!
Chase: Jungle bunny!
   Richard: Honky!
Chase: Spade!
   Richard: Honky! Honky!
Chase: Nigger!
   Richard: Dead honky!

Easiest sketch I ever write. All I do is bring out what is going on beneath the surface of that interview with Lorne and the NBC execs in the jai alai green room.

Meanwhile, I am monitoring Richard's drug intake. He's getting more and more cranked the closer we get to showtime. The whole cast is. I know the werewolf is going to come out, and I don't want to be collateral damage, so I get the fuck out of there and head back to California.

That Saturday, December 13, 1975, the bit kills when Richard and Chevy do it in front of the live studio audience. Even watching it on television, I can hear gasps and hollers in between the panicked laughter.

Richard's appearance puts *Saturday Night Live* on the map. It's a huge event, a water-cooler kind of success. Gil Scott-Heron does a great rendition of his antiapartheid anthem, "Johannesburg."

There are other bits, other sketches. We open the show with a plant in the audience standing up and saying, "I know who killed Kennedy!" Then, BANG!—a gunshot rings out, he drops dead, and we segue into Chevy Chase: "Live from New York, it's *Saturday Night!*" In another skit, Dan Aykroyd sees his whole family turn black on him.

For all the upheaval beforehand, the show actually appears smooth and tight. It's a miracle. NBC is stunned when they see that the rerun of the show the next spring actually scores a higher rating than the original. Word of mouth is that good.

But it's the job interview sketch that everyone talks about. It attains the status of comedy classic. It's like an H-bomb that Richard and I toss into America's consciousness. All that shit going on behind closed doors is now out in the open. There's no putting the genie back in the bottle.

The *N*-word as a weapon, turned back against those who use it, has been born on national TV. Together with *That*

Nigger's Crazy and his concert tour, Richard's *Saturday Night Live* guest-hosting appearance lends his career a terrifying kind of energy.

The boulder is rolling now. Bouncing downhill, smashing everything in its way. The Richard Pryor Celebrity Express picks up speed and momentum. I figure I have to make sure I do only two things. One, figure out some way to push it so that it gets going even faster. Two, avoid getting run over.

In a television studio in Burbank, we get the boulder rolling faster, all right, but it rolls over us at the same time.

THE SHOW

CHAPTER 21

At Ye Little Club in 1975 I see a vision of prettiness and strangeness stand up in front the crowd on open-mic night. She's scattered with nervousness and all over the place in her act, which features lots of high school humor. All I see are lips and a bone-thin body.

But there's something there. She's funny, for one thing. I mean the whole way she approaches the world is funny. The actual bits aren't quite there yet. But when you got that natural comic attitude, the lines will come sooner or later. I always think comedians are born, not made. It's something in our DNA.

The thin-as-a-rail woman closes her act with her introduction. "I'm Sandra Bernhard," she says, waving herself off the stage. I go over to her.

"Girl," I say, "you're a cigarette come to life."

She looks at me. "Thanks, I think," she says. She's twenty years old, a manicurist in Beverly Hills.

"The manicurist to the stars," she says, fluttering her hands in the air.

"I bet," I say. "You found your way here, so you have to be getting some inside information somewhere."

She's not a classic beauty. Then again, a lot of classic beauties aren't classic beauties. Like Bette Davis. Take a look at her and tell me you'd ever guess she was a movie star.

Ah, yes, "nigger lips." That's what they call Sandra all her life. They put her through hell in school. She tells me that people point and stare at her in airports as though she is a freak. As a teenager it makes her cry. She is the ugly duckling. Onstage, in front of a microphone, she becomes a swan.

I always love the underdog. So I start to take Sandra around. I take her to shows at army bases. I take her down to South Central, to Maverick's Flat and Redd Foxx's. Black folks go nuts for her. It's like magic. The first people to really get Sandra Bernhard are the audiences down on Crenshaw.

Richard comes to see her. "Boy, you can really pick them," he says. As a female, she doesn't get through to him because she's one of those rare women he doesn't want to fuck. But as a comic, he understands at once. She's a natural.

It's lucky for her that Richard likes her, because the next year is his breakout year in Hollywood. He finally gets what he's wanted all his life. When *Silver Streak* hits theaters, he's a movie star. On top of that, his new album, *Bicentennial Nigger*, sells even better than *That Nigger's Crazy* and wins Richard another Grammy.

The Shell oil company had commercials back then with the tag, "And that's the way it was." I get a T-shirt made that says, "Bicentennial Nigger: And dat's the way it wuz." Richard sees it and goes nuts, using it for the name of his album.

When you get to be a big dog in Hollywood, you see a lot of bones tossed your way. NBC offers Richard a chance to do his own Lily Tomlin–style comedy special, to be aired in the spring of 1977. Producer Rocco Urbisci develops the concept, and we pitch it with a question mark in the title—*The Richard Pryor Special?*—to set it apart from other shows, but also because we talk about mixing it up, putting a few dramatic skits in with the comedic riffs.

"Mr. Mooney, you do the casting shit," Richard tells me. He doesn't want to bother assembling the actors. For the big names, he pulls in a few favors, like getting John Belushi on, but mostly it is up to me. I feel like I am given the keys to the Cadillac.

I hire the most talented people I know. Sandra Bernhard is among them, in her first TV appearance. It's not much— just a small role of a token woman writer in a room full of black radicals—but it gets Sandra her AFTRA card.

The special itself is a mixed-bag of comedy and drama, just like Richard wanted. He wanders around the NBC Studios in Burbank, trying to scare up ideas for the show. He encounters one hard case after another. The first is LaWanda Page, fresh from playing Fred's nemesis on *Sanford and Son*. She does a church-lady riff as "Sister Mabel Williams."

The Sister Mabel sketch leads into Richard playing his donation-grubbing preacher character, Rev. James L. White, done up with a huge natural, white Crenshaw pumps, and gold-chain chest bling. A chorus of singers behind him sends up a chant of "Money" all through his appearance.

Richard and I come up with the punch line to the riff: When the phones on his religious telethon don't ring fast enough, Rev. White says it's because he's not getting the "crossover" money from white audiences. He announces that all the money received will be donated to the BTAM—the Back to Africa Movement, to send black folks back to their homeland. The switchboards immediately light up.

I get the Pips to come on, the same folks who used to crash at our Sunset Boulevard bungalow when I lived there with Carol. Gladys Knight herself isn't with them, but we make that the joke and have the backup singers do their same act without the lead. They do all their moves toward an empty microphone. It's funny and weird and meaningful all at the same time. Richard loves it because he thinks the special should be about bringing folks who are always in the background up to the fore.

My favorite line in the show comes when Richard encounters a thief named Booster Johnson. Richard is in a tuxedo, and Booster is in street clothes and a do-rag, but they find common ground.

"Just trying to stay three steps ahead," Booster says. "Because you know they're going to push you two back."

That's pure Oak-Town ghetto wisdom, right there, but it transfers well enough to Hollywood, to New York, to the wider world. White, black, red, yellow, or brown, those are words to live by.

All through the production of the special, Richard is chafing against NBC brass on the one side and his own private demons on the other. He is still sucking Smirnoff and snorting cocaine like a madman. It's funny, the special shows Richard roaming NBC's studios like they're his home turf, but in reality we feel like outsiders there.

The episode in the show where the security guard checks Richard's and Booster's names in his "black book" isn't that far from the truth. Heading for the commissary, I get shut out of Studio Two one afternoon without ID, and security won't let me back in until Richard sends someone to fetch me.

Richard likes to play it cool, as though he doesn't give a shit whether his special succeeds or fails, but the mask always slips. He's needy. He's afraid of disappointment. This all leads to his becoming a bundle of anxiety, which in turn leads to more coke and alcohol.

I know that sooner or later the stripped wires of Richard's manic energy and nervous stress are going to cross somewhere in his brain, and it will spark a meltdown. I tell him that his main stressor, one that he can't resolve, is that whenever he does something popular, he's afraid he's not keeping it real.

"I see it happen," I tell him. "The minute you hear white people applauding you, you get all pissed at yourself because you think you ain't being black enough."

He knows it's true, but he can't see a way out of the bind. The pressure doesn't let up when Richard's comedy special is a top-rated success, crossing over to black and white audiences both.

NBC offers Richard his own weekly comedy-variety show. They offer Richard what he calls "bad money"—so much cash that he can't refuse it: $2 million a year.

"What am I going to do, Mr. Mooney?"

I know him well enough to know he's not really asking. The answer is already clear. "You're gonna take the fucking money and run," I say.

"Those assholes at NBC'll never let me do my material," he says. "They'll mess with it until it's nothing but shit."

I don't argue with him, and as it turns out, Richard is right. We both find it easy to tell the future where TV executives are concerned. They are stupidly predictable.

Getting the NBC series, along with a small art-house movie role, ultimately leads Richard to the crash I have been expecting all along. It's like witnessing a slow-motion auto accident. Just as Richard takes me along with him as he becomes a star, when he spins out, I'm right there, too.

CHAPTER 22

Once again, Richard hands over the keys to the Caddy. He wants me to do all the casting for his comedy series (which, in a stroke of originality, NBC is calling *The Richard Pryor Show*). I begin by signing up some young comics I see at the Store or down at the Improv, a club that opens in the mid-1970s on Melrose.

The Store is my true playground. I am there almost every night. At about this time I start using a phrase in my act that spreads like wildfire all over the country. Whenever I catch some homeboy trying to front in some outrageous way, I have a two-word reality check for him: "Nigger, please."

Those two words have a lot of history to them. I think back on Mama. Whenever I say something that's obviously a lie, she just checks me with a look. Not quite a scowl, just an expression that immediately establishes that Mama ain't going to take not one bit of shit from a silver-tongued grandson like me.

Everybody raised by a black grandmama knows that look cold. It makes me smile just thinking about it. It's the "nigger, please" expression. *Yes, I know what you just said, I speak English, I recognize the words coming out of your mouth, but if you think for one single second I am going to buy any of that nonsense, you are out of your pea-picking mind.*

The *N* word in "nigger, please" is more of an identifier than a racial insult. What it's saying is, *Listen, we're all in the same community. We grew up on the same streets. We know all the scams, all the dodges, all the bullshit. So don't try to run none of that on me.* As I sometimes say, "I may have been born yesterday, but I stayed up all night, so I know something."

The reason "nigger, please" catches on so fast, the reason the phrase is revolutionary, is that it is the first time black-on-black criticism goes public. We are usually so careful to back up the brothers and protect the sisters in front of the white folks. The attitude is, We don't need to air our dirty linen in public. The white folks are going to cut us down with insults soon enough.

Between us, of course, the insults fly, the dozens go down, the long knives come out. Ain't nobody can call black people on their bullshit like a black person. But "nigger, please" drags that business into the open. It says, *See? We're strong enough to dish it and take it, we can give each other reality checks better than anyone. We're keeping it real.*

The phrase becomes the "Where's the beef?" of the black community. What's great is that even though white people have been feeling the sense of it for years, they can't say it anymore in public unless they're some cracker racist redneck who doesn't care if he gets a beatdown.

As soon as I start dropping the phrase into my show, it becomes a virus. The timing is weird, because during this period I'm traveling cross-country for the first time to appear at comedy clubs in New York—the Improv, Catch A Rising Star, and the Comic Strip Live. And when I start hanging out in the city, my trademark phrase starts showing up everywhere in my wake.

"Nigger, please." I hear it from the mouths of other comics in the clubs, on the streets, and in the subways. I should have copyrighted that shit. I could be retired on royalties.

I say it to Richard all the time. "I'm not feeling this comedy series, Mr. Mooney," he says. "It's gonna be shitty, shitty, shit-*tie!* The worst show ever on TV. I can't do it! I'm in a trap. I cannot do this shit!"

Nigger, please. Take the money and run with it.

Casting the series, I give Robin Williams his first television job, long before his appearances as Mork on *Happy Days* and his own starring role doing the same character on *Mork & Mindy*. I see Robin all the time at the Store. He and Richard are fucking the same waitress. I always like Robin's act, but I am not crazy about him the way other people are.

Happy Days producer Garry Marshall, who gives Robin his job as Mork, is the guy who usually gets credit for discovering him. Richard is there first, but anyone who is at the Store in those days knows Robin has great potential. I introduce him to Richard, and we use him on the series because he's funny and can do any part we send his way. We sign Sandra again, too.

Other people I sign up are Marsha Warfield, who goes on to play Roz on *Night Court,* "Detroit" Johnny Witherspoon, Tim Reid, and the comic who will go on to *Everybody Loves Raymond*, Brad Garrett. Garrett's young as shit when we hire him, not even twenty years old, just starting out, years away from winning *Star Search* and breaking out on *The Tonight Show.*

We work on the *Pryor Show* scripts up at Richard's house in Northridge, upstairs in the study. It's a big room with lots of chairs and couches, and overlooks the rest of the house and the mountains beyond. The whole arrangement makes it easy for Richard. He never has to be away from his comfort zone.

A stenographer sits there, taking down our every word, no matter how stupid. "Richard picks his nose—write that down!" Richard says, making the secretary his straight man. Rocco Urbisci, the producer, sits in, and some other writers, including David Banks, Richard's record producer. It's a classic spitball situation, with everybody throwing out ideas and seeing what sticks.

"Mr. Mooney's the only one telling me no," he shouts at everybody. "The rest of you sit there and motherfucking nod like a bunch of bobble-head dolls!"

His screaming at them makes no difference. They continue to suck up to the star. It makes for an uneven atmosphere, but eventually we come up with a thick sheaf of ideas for skits, sight gags, and parodies. Like he insisted on for the special, Richard wants a mix, not just comedy, but drama and even political sketches, too.

Not many people know it, but before she becomes the Clinton-inauguration poet laureate and Oprah's friend, Maya Angelou is a singer, dancer, and actress. She's already well known for writing *I Know Why the Caged Bird Sings*. I introduce her to Richard, who had never heard of her before.

We cast her to do a great dramatic riff, a black woman doing a monologue over the body of her passed-out drunken husband—Richard as a wino. Maya plays it straight, and even the first time we do it in rehearsal, it's great. I see women in tears afterward. Maya writes the monologue herself, and it gets to the soul of what goes on between black men and black women.

But all of a sudden, it looks as though the show is going nowhere. NBC tosses a wrench into the works by reneging on a clause in the contract. Richard demands that the show go on late, so we can do more adult-oriented bits. He even gets it in writing. But instead of scheduling the show after "family hour," NBC announces it as going on at 8 o'clock on Tuesday evening.

Richard freaks. He pulls the plug. *The Richard Pryor Show* is over before it ever gets started.

CHAPTER 23

One reason why Richard is all bent and moody during this time is he is just coming off a Paul Schrader movie, a drama that he's real proud of but that puts him through hell. Schrader is brilliant—he's the screenwriter for Scorsese's *Taxi Driver* and *Raging Bull*—but nobody could ever call him Mr. Sunshine.

The role Richard takes is Zeke in *Blue Collar,* where he's acting alongside Yaphet Kotto and Harvey Keitel. The production films in late spring 1977. The set is a pressure cooker. Schrader does nothing to cool it out.

"Dude likes tension on the set," Richard complains to me. "He thinks it will show up dramatically in the art of the movie."

Richard is miserable all through the shoot. He has fistfights with his costars, throwing punches at both Harvey and Yaphet on separate occasions. He flings scripts, props, and other stuff around the set.

Off the set, when I see him at night, he's drinking and doping like a real addict. He runs Amy, his drug mule, ragged. One evening, during a single six-hour period between six and midnight, he sends her out three times on resupply runs. I counted.

Not all of that shit is going up Richard's nose, since he's got a whole host of hangers-on to take care of, but a lot of it does. But he never bleeds, he never rots out his nostrils like a lot of coke hounds do. He's got a cast-iron septum.

When I finally see *Blue Collar,* I realize it's a great movie and that Richard is great in it. But I wonder if it is worth it. The shoot puts Richard through an emotional obstacle course. He feels as though he can never be friends with his costars again. Too much bullshit, too much bad blood. Richard comes off that movie shell-shocked. I think today we'd call it posttraumatic stress.

But the proof is in the pudding, and *Blue Collar* is a dramatic role that Richard's proud of. The box office is lousy, but reviews are good. A critic for the *LA Times* calls it a triumph.

"Many more motherfucking triumphs like that," Richard says, "and I'll be dead."

No rest for the wicked. Right on the heels of *Blue Collar* comes the bullshit surrounding *The Richard Pryor Show.* Richard tells NBC they're not honoring the contract that calls for the network to put the show on after family hour, so he's walking out.

Richard's moves are never simple. There's never just one reason behind his decisions. Part of the face-off over the show is Richard's refusing to get pushed around by corporate types. But another part of it is that he's afraid he's going to bomb.

Stalemate. All of us who got cranked up to do the show are expecting paychecks. But they're not coming. Some fools on the crew go out and hire an airplane to fly over Richard's house in the Valley, trailing a banner that reads SURRENDER RICHARD, as if that would change his mind.

In the middle of this Richard flies to Europe with his family. He's got four kids living with him, and a new wife, Deborah. The trip is supposed to be a vacation to get Richard away from the stresses of Hollywood. But he's not used to acting the family man. He comes back from vacation needing a vacation.

But the break gives him some perspective. Richard suggests a compromise on the show—four episodes, instead of the ten called for in the contract. What can the network do? Everybody wants a piece of Richard. Four shows isn't as good as ten, but it's better than nothing.

From our experience with *The Richard Pryor Special?*, we know we're going to run up against the NBC censors, so we come up with a beautiful sight gag to open the show. Richard comes on, shot from the head up, and swears to the camera he will never be compromised, he's going to be just as edgy and controversial as ever.

"I've given up absolutely nothing to be on network TV," he says. The camera pulls out to show his full body. Richard is naked and dickless.

The gag is done with a bodysuit, so he isn't nude at all, but it is still too much for NBC. They hate the criticism, but they use the "nudity" excuse to kill the bit.

Richard is furious, but the censorship backfires on NBC. The controversy shows up on all the network news broadcasts. Many more people see the sketch on the news than ever watch the show. I have a good laugh about it, but Richard doesn't see it as funny. He's too angry at NBC to see that the controversy just makes people love him more.

"See how that shit works? NBC gets all the free publicity. Those motherfuckers always win," he says. That's how Richard sees it. The way I see it is that we're starting to kick down the walls of Fortress Hollywood brick by brick, gag by gag—"just trying to stay three steps ahead because you know they're going to push you back two."

On the set, Richard swings from highs to lows like some sort of bipolar crazy person. The werewolf comes out repeatedly. The ensemble cast I put together never knows who they're going to get when they approach him. He places himself under enormous pressure. I feel as though it's too much for him, as though he's going to explode and wind up, like he warns me again and again, "with a bullet in my head."

I don't "nigger, please" him when he says shit like that. It scares me.

But despite all the tension on the set, we produce some of the best television ever broadcast. The Maya Angelou bit comes off beautifully, unbelievably good. Nothing like it has ever been shown before or since.

I get to act in a Chaplin-style pantomime bit with Richard—no dialogue, just music on the soundtrack. He plays Mr. Fix-It, and I am his customer, with a broken-down car. In a series of sight gags, Richard totally demolishes the car. At the end, miracle of miracles, he manages to start the wreck's engine. Overjoyed, he leaps out to shake my hand. My arm falls off.

It's the purest form of comedy, a sketch that would play in Thailand just as well as in Oakland. You don't need words. I treasure it as one of the highest achievements of my life, to share a stage with my best friend Richard, just me and him, making people laugh.

Other sketches are less stripped-down. A parody of the bar scene in *Star Wars* has Richard as a bartender keeping a rowdy crowd of aliens in check. It reminds me of him trying to keep the ensemble of actors and writers on track, trying to keep it real. Richard loves *Star Wars*. He's obsessed with it. He tells me because the characters are from a galaxy "far, far away," then they can't be prejudiced.

Richard does a samurai skit that shows off his obsession with all things Asian. He and Robin Williams slip a cocaine-snorting reference into an Egyptian tomb-of-the-pharaohs sketch. Racial politics keep creeping into the content of the show. There's a lot of Afrocentric material, because Richard is getting more and more interested in Africa. African dances, glorification of the black female, a voodoo skit where Richard attempts to heal Robin's crippled arm.

In another bit, more than three decades before Obama, Richard acts as the "Fortieth President of the United States" at a press conference. He starts the sketch solemn enough, but becomes increasingly raucous, calling only on black reporters while telling the white journalist from Mississippi to sit down. He appoints our old Oakland friend Huey P. Newton as the head of the FBI.

I do the audience warm-up for the show, because Richard doesn't trust anyone else. Not only do I perform multiple functions on the show, I go home with Richard and buck him up during his dangerous moods. I have the professional and the personal at the same time.

By the fourth show, Richard has had it. He's ready to bail. It's clear from the ratings that NBC won't be interested in going forward. We're scheduled up against the two top-rated shows on TV back then, *Happy Days* and *Laverne & Shirley*. We barely dent their numbers. No one has succeeded in mounting a new TV variety show for years, and we don't break that trend.

In public, Richard talks about his inability to work under the rules of network censorship. It's a good story, and everyone in the media buys into it. But from the inside, I know the truth. Richard can't stand the demands of a weekly TV show. It's the pressure, the drugs, the obligations. He can't handle it. So he uses the "censorship" excuse to slide out of it. The explanation has just enough truth to it that it's widely accepted, even today.

Richard and I charged Fortress Hollywood and got shut down. The show crashed. We got flattened.

I have a big hand in the failed show, from casting to writing. So why am I happy? I swear that my life could end right there, laughing with my best friend on national TV, and I would be cool with it. I don't let any of the stresses of the show weigh on me the way Richard does. He goes into a deep funk. He's the biggest star in Hollywood, but in his own mind, he's a failure.

CHAPTER 24

As Richard retreats to Northridge to lick his wounds (and lick the coke crumbs off the mirror), I get my own taste of the big screen.

Growing up, people tell me all the time that I look like Sam Cooke. I don't think I look like anybody but me, but I take it as a compliment to be compared to the greatest soul singer of all time. That resemblance, coupled with my increased visibility on *The Richard Pryor Show,* leads to my first costarring role in a movie, playing Sam Cooke, with Gary Busey as the lead, in *The Buddy Holly Story.*

At the start of his rock-and-roll career, Buddy Holly tours with Cooke. He and the Crickets are always being confused for a black act when people hear their records without seeing the band onstage. Buddy Holly sounds pretty white-bread today, but it's a measure of how much white musicians lift from black music that everyone thinks he is black back then.

Holly and the Crickets are booked at the Apollo, and the crowd gasps when the curtains rise to reveal a white band.

"We didn't expect you, either," Holly says, before proceeding to win over the all-black audience with his music.

In one of my scenes with Busey, I manage to slip in a time-honored insult joke straight out of the dozens:

> *Me (as Sam Cooke):* Hey, young blood, I hear Solly booked you for the whole tour.
> *Gary Busey (as Buddy Holly):* Yeah, I couldn't stand seeing you and my poker money leaving town.
> *Cooke:* Come on back here, we'll play another hand— for that suit you're wearing. I want to give it to my brother. He's an undertaker. [*laughter*]
> *Holly:* Get your money out, Cooke!

But the scene that really kills for me is when Cooke and his bandmate Luthor (played by Matthew Beard, famous for playing Stymie in *The Little Rascals*) try to check into a blacks-only segregated hotel with white-boy Buddy Holly and the Crickets in tow. The group engages in some high-spirited fronting with the black desk clerk. The scene plays out in a way worthy of a sketch on *The Richard Pryor Show*.

> *Hotel desk clerk:* Mr. Cooke! Always glad to have you. [*He sees Buddy Holly and the Crickets*] Mr. Cooke, you know this is a restricted hotel?
> *Cooke:* You mean there is no room for my entourage?
> *Hotel desk clerk [misunderstanding the word entourage]:* Oh, yeah, we've got plenty of room out there for your car—you can park anywhere out there.
> *Luthor:* No, no, my good man—entourage. You see, these three young men of the Caucasian persuasion, why, they happen to be Mr. Cooke's personal valets.

They fulfill his every need. So therefore they must
have rooms next to his.

Hotel desk clerk: Mr. Cooke, you mean to tell me you
have three white valets?

Cooke: That is correct.

*Charles Martin Smith (as Crickets drummer Ray Bob
Simmons):* Mr. Cooke, will you need your bath immediately or after your rubdown?

Cooke: Not now, boy.

Hotel desk clerk: Mr. Cooke, I like your style! You can
sign in right here, you and your entourage.

Turnabout is fair play. I know my American history. I recognize this scene to be the exact flip side of Sam Cooke getting
turned away from the segregated Holiday Inn in my old hometown of Shreveport, Louisiana. Believe me, I pronounce my
last line of the scene—"Not now, boy!"—with a lot of energy.

Working on the big Columbia Pictures production im-
merses me once again in the boring but enjoyable atmosphere
on a film set. In contrast to the pressure cooker that Richard
experienced with *Blue Collar,* it's a relaxed, stress-free atmosphere. I get along with everyone, especially the Teamsters
on the crew, even play a little poker with Gary Busey and
the other actors.

While I'm on set, Richard phones me with the news that
he has had a heart attack. "Just a small one," he says. "But
you know what, Paul? Even a small heart attack is one hell of
a motherfucker." I can hear in his voice that Richard is
drinking and drugging as much as ever.

Just after *The Buddy Holly Story* wraps, I step into a
ruckus out at Richard's Northridge estate. In the early morning of New Year's Day 1978, Yvonne and I are at a party
there when I see the pentagram start to glow on Richard's

forehead. He's drinking and drugging. I know the werewolf is about to come out.

"Let's go," I say to Yvonne. "There's going to be some shit happening here."

Sure enough, later that night, my phone rings. Bleary-eyed and half asleep, I answer it.

"Mooney?" A voice comes over the telephone. "You got to get up here quick. Richie's shot up the whole damn place and the cops came."

It's a young dancer I know, a friend of Richard's wife, Deborah. By the time I get there, the damage has already been done. Richard and Deborah have never been the most serene couple, and early that morning, after staying up all New Year's Eve night partying, they get into it good. Richard chases Deborah and her friends out of the house, and then, to stop them from driving off, he rams their Buick with his Mercedes.

Just for good measure, he goes back into the house and gets his pride and joy *Dirty Harry* gun, a .357 revolver with Magnum loads, just like the one Clint Eastwood carries in the movie, only Richard's has a long-target barrel.

Richard has been getting more and more volatile lately, and more and more into guns. He has always kept pistols around the house, and sometimes they figure into unfortunate incidents.

As far back as *The Mack,* his 1973 pimp movie with the tagline "They're doing the job the cops can't!" he just misses getting busted for illegal possession of firearms. His girlfriend at the time finds Richard in bed with an actress from the film, and chases her naked ass out of Richard's house wielding one of his pistols. So weapons are not a new addition to the Pryor household.

But now he's got a whole arsenal, mostly handguns, but rifles and shotguns, too. Paranoia, drugs, and firearms—it's a bad combination. Richard unloads the .357 into Deborah's Buick, shooting out its tires, its windshield and windows, and putting a couple of thumb-size holes in the door panels. By this time Deborah and her friends have run screaming down the driveway, and soon enough the boys in blue arrive. They book Richard for assault.

A few hours later, Deborah is back at the house. She has her dancer friend call me. She's afraid the police are going to return and search the house. She wants me to come up to Northridge and hide Richard's arsenal.

Richard never lays a hand on a woman when I am around. It's like he is afraid of my judgment. Then again, when I see the werewolf in Richard about to come out, I know enough to get gone. So I'm never present to witness him turn violent. But I see evidence enough that he abuses his wives and girlfriends horribly. I hear the stories, some from Richard's own mouth.

Richard is like a train on twin tracks—with one rail ripped up and the other smooth. His personal life is a shambles. Deborah divorces him—the end of marriage number three. His professional life cruises along, clickety-clack. He does movies one after another, most of them bombs, like *The Wiz* and *California Suite*—but Richard is usually the best thing in them.

White people don't like anyone messing with their icons. *The Wizard of Oz* is like comfort food for white people, something familiar from their childhoods. It's sacred. When Diana Ross, Michael Jackson, and Richard show up on-screen doing the black version of *The Wizard of Oz*, white America turns its back. Nobody fucks with Dorothy and Toto.

But I know my history. I know that in the first movie version of the book, the silent film version from 1925, a black man named Snowball is going to the Wizard for his freedom. But the flying monkeys must have somehow gotten to Snowball before Judy Garland ever eased on down the yellow brick road.

While he's getting paid millions of dollars to act in bad movies, Richard's personal life gets jolted again when his grandmother Marie, the woman who raised him, dies from a stroke. Richard is with her in Peoria when she goes. He falls apart. I know how much she means to him. I've seen him with his mama when she comes out to visit. She's a strong woman, and Richard is even more of a child when she's around.

When he loses her, he turns to the bottle and the spoon, his constant companions. He's got a new girlfriend, a white actress named Jennifer Lee, who helps him through his depression over Marie's death. I try to stabilize him by giving him the only advice I know how to give: "You have to get back in front of the microphone," I say. "Stand-up, man—it's the only place a black man in America can really be free."

Just like he does after his Berkeley exile with *That Nigger's Crazy,* Richard takes my advice. He goes out on tour. Not only that but he takes a movie crew with him and films one of his concerts. The result is the man at his best: *Richard Pryor: Live in Concert.*

When his concert film is released in February 1979, Richard gets what he has always wanted. He's the star of the top-grossing movie in the country. *Live in Concert* even beats out *Superman* at the box office. He's "Super-Nigger" after all. His dream of being a successful movie star happens in a way he never imagines—through his stand-up act—but at least it finally comes through for him. He has achieved his ultimate goal. Anyone else is the world would be happy, relaxed, satisfied.

Not Richard.

CHAPTER 25

All through the 1970s at the Comedy Store, I'm tight with Mitzi Shore. I genuinely like the woman. And Mitzi loves me right back. She tells young comics who are just coming up, "You want to learn about comedy, watch Paul." She gives me lots of sets. Whenever I want to work the Store, it's there for me. I'm one of Mitzi's regulars.

But she and I have one area of serious disagreement. "Mitzi," I tell her, "slavery is dead. You got to start paying the comics."

I don't even say, "You have to start paying me." I don't put it that way, even though I am still hardscrabbling and I could use the money. I put it in terms she can relate to—namely, looking out for her own best interests. If you don't support these young comics, I tell her, you will have a rebellion on your hands.

Mitzi is stubborn about it. No way, she says. She's got this idea in her head that we are all some big comedy commune, and the Store provides a service: a place for comics to work out their routines. I think somewhere in her mind Mitzi believes the comics should be paying her for the privilege of time in front of a microphone.

On most nights, Mitzi perches like a hawk on the cashier's chair at the entrance of the Store, a tiny, thin, pale woman with straggly black hair. She dispenses her trademark gifts of cigarettes and bubble gum. She's effusive with support and encouragement. She loves mothering the comics. Half of them do dead-on impressions of Mitzi's nasal voice.

She gives love, but that's it. She refuses to toss even a small coin into the begging bowls of the performers who are filling her club with paying customers.

Make that "clubs," plural. Mitzi has built the Store into an empire. She's got a Comedy Store West, located near UCLA in Westwood, and one in San Diego. I'm seeing all this prosperity and success, and I'm thinking, this ain't right. How much money are we making for this woman, working for free?

It's a thing we comics talk about among ourselves, trying to total up the money coming in and the money going out. The door charge back then is $4.50. And the Store is packing them in—fifty to a hundred in the Original Room, a couple hundred in the Main Room. That's a thousand-plus per night just on door fees, never mind the drink tabs.

What would it take to pay the comics? There are maybe a hundred or a hundred fifty regulars who work the Store at least once a month. Twelve sets a night in the Original Room. If they rotate to all the rooms, there can be three or four dozen comedians working every night. Say Mitzi paid a bare-bones minimum of $5 for a set. She's still clearing a thousand dollars every night on the cover charges alone.

"Mitzi, give them something," I tell her over and over. "Give them five dollars a set."

She folds her arms across her chest and digs in her heels. No way.

I argue with her. I know how messy the beef will get if it goes public. "Let's settle this whole thing among ourselves, in the house," I say. "Nobody goes to the press, no big blow-ups. If this shit ever gets out on the street, we'll never get over it."

"No, Paul," Mitzi says. "That's not the way it works." That is her main line that she repeats again and again. *That's not the way it works.*

"Well, it ain't working this way, either. You are going to have a comic riot on your hands. There will be comedians splattered all over Sunset Strip. Their blood will be on your hands."

Mitzi reminds me of a rich woman who is getting alimony from her ex. She doesn't need it, but she's like a she-bear going after it. Her only reason for doing it is because she can.

In those days, comics call up the Store every evening to find out if they are scheduled that night. It's hard on the nerves. The performers are like court jesters, waiting on the favors of a queen.

I talk to the comics. Back then, people like Gary Shandling, Robin Williams, Michael Keaton, David Letterman, Johnny Dark, Elayne Boosler, and Jay Leno are Store regulars. I know that things are coming to a head, so I go back to Mitzi about it. I keep the tone light, but I hock her constantly. At first, she doesn't budge. When she does, she just makes things worse.

In 1977, Mitzi opens the big Main Room with professional Vegas-style comics, her ex-husband Sammy's people, Jackie Mason, Shelley Berman, and Mort Sahl, those types. Mitzi wants the Main Room to be a nightclub, like a casino lounge, so she pays them. But the Vegas comics would much rather work Vegas. So in fall 1978, Mitzi books the Main Room with the most popular of her regulars. Letterman and Leno both pack them in, filling the three-hundred-seat space.

Mitzi doesn't pay them a dime. She's not used to paying the young crop of comics who she has nurtured and workshopped. Just because they're booked in the Main Room, she doesn't see why she should change her ways.

That's it, I figure. That's where we draw the line. I reach out to the other comics. I go to everybody. "Shelley Berman works the Main Room," I say, "and he draws half crowds, but he gets all the money from the door. Then Dave or Jay come in and pack the place, and they get nothing? What kind of shit is that?"

I tell Mitzi that the rebellion I warned her about has arrived. Leno and Letterman are furious. Mitzi backs down. Okay, she says, anyone in the Main Room gets a share of the door. But the cat has been let out of the bag. We're calling ourselves Comedians for Compensation now, and we turn down Mitzi's compromise. Just like I warned her, once the beef gets out on the street, it turns ugly.

In March 1979, I help organize a meeting, getting a hundred angry comics together in one room. The result is chaos, like a clown convention. Everybody yells at once. I wonder if this is going to work. Comics cooperating? A disunion union?

Miraculously, we get our shit together. We bring in a figurehead white boy, Tom Dreesen, a comic and a former union guy, to be the public face of the strike. We organize picket lines, carrying signs that read THE YUK STOPS HERE and NO MONEY AIN'T FUNNY.

Richard supports the strike and even comes out with me

to the picket line. Jimmie Walker, a former Store regular and a huge star from his show *Good Times,* backs us up, too. Garry Shandling starts out with us but eventually crosses the picket line to perform after Mitzi offers $25 a set for weekends only. And Howie Mandel never honors the strike at all.

"You're working, so what do you care about this?" Howie asks me one night as I'm on the picket line.

"I care because it's about us," I say. "The comics." He stares at me blankly. It's like trying to explain slavery to a white man. He gets it, but not really. Howie walks past me into the Store. I channel Miss Amerae and level a silent curse at him, wishing that all his hair will fall out and he'll wind up hosting a stupid game show.

It is Jay Leno who finally turns the tide. I am out on the picket line every night that spring, mostly alongside my main man Detroit Johnny Witherspoon, who before the strike acts as the emcee for the Store. The two of us are there when one of the strikebreakers pulls his car into the driveway of the Store's parking lot. Blocked by the picket line, the scab bulls his car forward, and Leno does a pratfall backward. I can tell Jay is taking a fake showbiz flop, but it looks bad enough, and people freak.

Mitzi is at her usual post, watching the picket line from her big bay window in the Store. I don't know if she sees Leno fall down, but she finally caves. She agrees to pay all comics who appear at the Store $25 per set.

The strike ends, and most us go back to work, but the bad blood still flows. Mitzi feels betrayed. She freezes out some of the most active strikers. I get a pass because I tried to talk to her about it before the walk-out went down. She admits me back into her good graces. She's Mitzi the Mom again.

But not everybody feels the love. A comic named Steve Lubetkin thinks Mitzi has blackballed him. He's not getting sets. He goes into a funk. He climbs up to the roof of the Continental Hyatt, right next door to the Store, and jumps off, landing on the ramp to the club's parking lot after a fourteen-floor fall. His suicide note reads, "My name is Steve Lubetkin. I used to work at the Comedy Store."

I know Steve. I don't believe his suicide has anything to do with the Store. He is always on the edge. If it isn't the strike that sends him over, then it's something else.

The night he jumps, I'm at the Roxy, doing a show. I head to the Store afterward. They tell me a comic jumped, but they get the name wrong, another Steve, a guy I know just got a nose job.

"Are you sure?" I say. "A guy who just got a nose job won't mess it up by jumping off a building." I was right. It was the wrong Steve.

CHAPTER 26

The night Richard burns himself up I am at a club in Long Beach. I get the news later, from Mitzi at the close of my first set, four hours after the fire happens. It's past midnight when I drive up to Sherman Oaks Hospital.

"It's the pipe," I tell Mitzi. "It's the motherfucking base pipe."

Richard has always smoked coke, even way back. But the whole elaborate freebasing procedure only comes into play big-time at the end of the 1970s. He soaks the raw cocaine in some sort of solvent, usually 200-proof grain alcohol or 151 rum. Then he burns off the impurities. What's left is a rock of pure coke. He smokes that, and he gets a high that he loves more than life.

When I show up in Sherman Oaks, there's already a clusterfuck of media vans parked around the hospital. The reporters are like hungry wolves. They howl for any scrap of information. "Mooney! Mooney! Paul!" yell a few who recognize me as I run the gauntlet. Then the ones who don't know me take up the call. "Mooney! Mooney!"

Richard is actually at the burn center across the street from the hospital. Inside, a collection of friends and relatives gathers in a private lounge. As soon as I walk in, I get hit with it. *Omigod,* I think, *this is a death watch.* Jim Brown is there, and Richard's Aunt Dee, both of whom are at the house when Richard ignites himself. Jennifer Lee, his main woman at the time, is shut out from the inner circle for some reason, but she talks to me.

I am in total shock. I'm freaked out. I think my friend is dead. I'm like a zombie.

It's a time of rumors. I sort out the truth, mostly by talking to Jim. Richard shut himself in his master bedroom at around eight o'clock that evening. Fifteen minutes later, there's a loud pop and Richard comes tearing ass out of the room, smoking and on fire.

Aunt Dee stamps out the flames in the bedroom and dashes after Richard. He has run out of the house, down the driveway, and out onto the street, trying to outdistance his demons. His whole upper body is messed up. He's got a melted piece of his polyester shirt stuck to his chest.

Aunt Dee doesn't catch up to him until he's a full mile from the house, down Parthenia Street and onto Hayvenhurst. A couple of LAPD traffic cops are with him. They get involved because the sight of a burning movie star has naturally stopped traffic. But Richard doesn't want to quit. He runs until the ambulance comes. They have to toss a medicated sheet around him, one they use for burn victims, to get him to stop.

He's got third-degree burns over the top half of his body. The doctors give him a one-in-three chance to live.

Whenever a friend falls sick or gets hurt, all I want to know is what happened. It's like knowing the details will help somehow. It never does, really, but that's always my first reaction. What happened? Give me chapter and verse. That first night all we hear are rumors. Richard's brain-dead. Drug dealers set him on fire. I know the truth. It is the pipe. I know it before anyone tells me.

I see him only days later, when the risk of infection has lessened and they allow him visitors. He ain't all bandaged up, because they have to let the burns air out. He's lying in a special burn-victim bed. It's too early for the doctors to apply the skin grafts.

I walk in and I say, "Dr. Frankenstein."

I start laughing. Richard starts laughing. I can tell it hurts him to laugh, but he does it anyway.

"Dr. Frankenstein," I say, "the operation did not succeed." We both laugh our asses off.

All through the month of June, I visit him almost every day. Jim Brown is there, nearly camped out, and an actor friend of Richard's named Stan Shaw, who he met on the set of a Motown production about black baseball, *The Bingo Long Traveling All-Stars and Motor Kings*. Richard's ex-wives—Deborah and Shelley—are around, too. Jennifer Lee remains an outcast because Richard believes she told the police he had been freebasing.

He *had* been freebasing, of course, but he doesn't want the Gestapo LAPD to know it. The rum that he is using to burn the impurities from the coke ignites the fire that burns him. In those days, half of Los Angeles is freebasing. It's like the new thing.

I tell all my black friends to stay away from freebasing. I know that with the word "free" in it, it's not for us.

Everybody in Richard's inner circle always uses the same word. *Accident.* As in, "I heard about the accident from . . ." "He was in serious danger of infection right after the accident . . ." "It's been a week since the accident . . ."

I go along, but I don't buy it. I've seen too much of Richard's behavior to believe in accidents. The man's been committing slow-motion suicide ever since I've known him, and suddenly he has an accident? Drug use of the kind Richard indulges in is always suicidal, pure and simple. Or impure and unsimple.

Every time Richard makes an insane, messed-up move, I always respond by saying the same thing. I say it when he shoots up Deborah's car, and I say it when he won't rest after his heart attack. I wind up saying it to Richard at least a half dozen times over the course of our friendship.

"Stop trying to rush death," I tell him. "Just wait. It's coming to you. You don't have to rush it."

How does that rum get all over Richard? Does he spill it on himself by "accident"? Or is he totally psychotic and pours it over his own head before lighting himself on fire? Whether it is a spill or a pour that sets him ablaze, Richard's trying to kill himself up there alone in his master bedroom in Northridge. He's trying to commit suicide.

I don't tell anyone this at the burn center, and I sure as hell don't talk to anyone like Jim Brown about it, but I have my own private theory about the fire.

Richard wants to burn himself black.

I've never seen anyone more messed up over success than Richard Pryor. For him, it's a constant battle between success in the white world and keeping it real for his black self.

Richard is more successful than ever. Deep in his mind, that means he's more white than ever. He can't fight his way out of this bind. He loves the money, he loves the approval and women and celebrity, but it costs him his soul. So he lights himself on fire. He's freebasing himself, burning off the white impurities. He figures he can only be real if he's a cinder. Let Hollywood try to cast him then.

When shrinks talk to suicidal people who have survived their attempts, you know what they find? They talk to a leaper, say, one who lands on an awning or something and somehow survives. The leaper says, "You know, doc, as soon as I jumped out that fourteenth-floor window, I had this overpowering thought. 'I don't want to die.'"

Steve Lubetkin probably has that same thought as he's tumbling down off the Continental Hyatt to the Comedy Store parking lot. I know Richard has that thought as soon as the flames engulf him. That's why he runs. He decides he wants to live after all.

The LAPD traffic cops who first approach ask him to stop running. "I can't," Richard says. "If I stop, I'll die."

CHAPTER 27

Richard's in the burn center, and I'm back and forth visiting him all the time. The problem is, when we're together, we can't help ourselves from cracking each other up. We cannot not laugh.

Say that Richard in another lifetime is hiding in the river thicket from the Klan, and he knows that if they hear him, he's one lynched black man. But he sees a doodlebug that looks at him funny and he laughs out loud. He's discovered and strung up by the Klan, all because it is impossible for him to keep a laugh inside.

He laughs more than anyone I ever meet. His laughter is as contagious as a goddamn hospital. When I am with him, everything is funny. A fat man bending over a sandwich case at a deli, sticking his big ass out a mile wide into the aisle, cracks us up. Everything's funny.

When Richard is recovering in Northridge, I tell him a joke. I light a match and pass it in the air in front of me. "What's this?" I ask him. He shakes his head, but he looks as though he knows what's coming. "Richard Pryor running."

He stares at me out of that scarred face. His lips and one ear are all burned, he's getting grafts off his legs and ass to transfer skin to his upper body. He looks at me and, even in the sorry shape he's in, he laughs. He laughs because it's funny. Sick, but funny.

I witness Richard's toughness during his burn treatments, procedures where the dead skin has to be scrubbed off with a rough sponge. It's one of the most painful procedures in all of medicine. Richard bears up under it. When I talk to him, it's like a paradox. He's as happy as I've seen him in a long while. He can't drink and drug, so those demons are laid to rest, at least for a little while. He is full of future plans.

He wants to tell his life story in a movie. He wants to do it all, growing up in Peoria, the chitterling circuit, the marriages, Hollywood. "I want you to help me write it, Paul," he says.

I tell him what he should do is a children's show. He needs a new image after the fire, as far away from drugs and freebasing as he can get. "You think they'll let me?" he asks. On the face of it, Richard hosting a children's show is not a slam dunk. People know him for his mouth, with "motherfucker" coming out of it every other second. And they know him as the star who lit himself on fire with the rum he was using as a freebasing solvent.

But kids love Richard. In almost every episode of *The Richard Pryor Show*, we have a kid's segment. He's a child himself, so he has a natural rapport with children. And actually, the top-grossing Richard Pryor film, beating out even *Silver Streak*, is *The Muppet Movie*, where he has a cameo as a balloon vendor.

CBS loses their long-running Saturday morning kid's cartoon from Bill Cosby, *Fat Albert*, so they sign on for *Pryor's Place*. It's an inner-city *Sesame Street*–style live-action thing with puppets, and we have a good time writing characters for it. My favorite is Chill the musician, who Richard plays in his finest rasta jazzman style. The theme song has a funk groove: "Whoa, oh, let's get on over to Pryor's Place/Whoa, oh, we're gonna party so don't be late."

In later days, when he is back at the bottle, the pipe, and the cigarettes, I hear Richard singing the chorus of that children's song as he pulls the mirror toward him. He gives me a sly sideways look and laughs. I'm probably the only one present who knows where that line comes from. The rest of the people Richard parties with never get up before noon, so they would never have seen *Pryor's Place*.

But our real work in those days is always on Richard's biopic. Rocco Urbisci, Richard and I settle into his upstairs office, just down the hall from the bedroom where he set himself on fire, and write the script together. Even though I learned to type in high school, it's easier for us to have a stenographer in the room. It's how we work on the *Pryor Show*, and that's how we work now. We fling bits around, situations and one-liners, trying to crack each other up. The stenographer lady has a hard time keeping up. If we can make her laugh, we know we're in the right place.

Richard is golden in Hollywood because of his concert films. *Richard Pryor: Live on Sunset Strip* and *Richard Pryor: Here and Now* both hit big. Audiences are still looking for the same laughs they found when they watched *Live in Concert*. People love them some Richard Pryor, but they love him best only one way—behind the microphone. His dramatic features, like *The Toy* (his comeback film after the suicide attempt), don't do as well.

His pet project through all this is the movie of his life. What comes out of our script sessions is *Jo Jo Dancer, Your Life Is Calling*. We come up with a freaky way to put the film

On set: The producer Rocco Urbisci, Richard, and me during the filming of *Jo Jo Dancer*

together, approaching it as though Richard is cut loose from time, drifting through episodes of his life while he lies dying from burning himself up.

It's some of the bravest shit I've ever seen anyone do on film. During the shoot, Richard puts himself through the whole fire episode again. The audience actually gets to witness his suicide attempt on-screen, watch him pour the rum over his head, see him light himself on fire.

Watching him act out that scene in *Jo Jo Dancer,* I am floored by the level of pain Richard had to be feeling in order to do something so extreme. That is some horrible misery he is in. It's like he wants to transfer the emotional pain inside of him to physical pain on the outside. When he's all scarred up and burnt to shit, we get to see what it's like on the inside of Richard's skin.

Not all the scenes are as scarifying as the fire. My favorite parts of the movie are the childhood episodes in the whorehouse in Peoria. Richard has so much juice in Hollywood that he packs up the whole production to film on location in his old hometown.

I put a lot of myself into *Jo Jo,* too. In the scene at the whorehouse where Richard's mama talks to her friend the psychic, I name the friend Miss Amerae and give her the vibe of my own mama's voodoo-spell-casting best friend.

Once again, Richard hands over casting duties to me. I bring in one of my favorite singers, Carmen McRae. Billy Eckstein plays another singer, one with whom the young comic Jo Jo shares a burlesque-show stage. The beautiful Dianne Abbot, Robert DeNiro's wife, plays Jo Jo's mother. Paula Kelly acts the part of Richard's fantasy figure, the Satin Doll, the hooker with a heart of gold, the same character we also put into his TV special. There's a montage sequence tracked by Richard's Berkeley theme song, "What's Going On," which plays over street scenes and Jo Jo's rise as a comic.

But it's all too close to the bone. Scoey Mitchell is Jo Jo's father, who puts him down with the exact words Richard heard from LeRoy Pryor during his youth: "This boy ain't shit and his mama ain't shit, either!"

We watch Richard rob his way out of a mob nightclub, destroy the car of one of his wives ("That car's going to need a tune-up," cracks his alter ego character, after Richard drives the Cadillac off a cliff), and crawl on his hands and knees trying to pick bits of rock cocaine out of the carpet in his bedroom.

Richard and I get to write his obituary in *Jo Jo Dancer*. In the last scene, he puts on his preacher-man voice and does a stand-up riff around his own funeral, pretending to gaze down at his own burnt-up corpse.

He tore his ass on the freeway of life. The boy was a mess. He run through life like shit run through a goose. And now he rests here with a smile on his face. I guess that's a smile. I hope that's his face. You sure that isn't his ass? It look like his ass! Some people lead with their chin. Life kind of forces you to do that—to lead with your chin. But this man here, he led with his nuts. If his nuts wasn't in a vise, he wasn't happy.

Only Richard could burn himself up and still be able to crack jokes about how his ass resembles his face. When we're writing the script, I keep thinking I am going too far, that Richard will draw the line somewhere. He never does. That's some ballsy shit. Richard is fearless all the way through *Jo Jo Dancer,* confronting the episodes of his life that dog him. Nuts in a vise.

This boy ain't shit! That line has to be what is echoing somewhere in Richard's head, right at the moment when he pours 151-proof rum over himself. It's an awful curse to give to a young child. As fucked-up as Richard is from his childhood—and his craziness runs long and deep—I always think the real miracle is that he can laugh at his life at all.

CHAPTER 28

Yvonne wants her own business, so I set her up in a juice bar way down on the eastern end of Sunset. We call it Mooney's Juices Plus, and we name all the drinks after everyone we know. The Richard Pryor. The Rick James. The Eddie Murphy. We throw a grand opening, but Richard doesn't show up.

He's pissed off because I didn't tell him ahead of time that I was planning on opening the spot—like a child, jealous of secrets being kept from him. The whole juice-bar business represents something in my life that he doesn't know about. I don't mean to spring it on him, but I'm busy, and it just happens. It's Yvonne's thing. It reminds me of the time Yvonne and I buy a brand-new Cadillac. When we drive up to Northridge in it to see Richard, he reacts as though we've somehow pissed him off by not telling him about the car beforehand. I think he feels his life is out of control enough as it is. He doesn't need surprises from his friends.

But Mooney's juice bar does okay without Richard's help. A lot of Hollywood folk come by to buy. Denzel Washington, Debbie Allen, Rick James, Diahann Carroll, and Bette Midler

Healthy business: Yvonne in our shop in Hollywood, Mooney's Juices

are all customers. But in the same way it happens for a lot of couples, the new business marks the end of my marriage to Yvonne. It's like a cliché. Start a new business, move into a new house—sure enough, it'll bust up your relationship.

Yvonne and I used to live near a rich white couple who have broken up but still live together. They're separated, but friends. She lives upstairs in their house, he lives downstairs. They invite us over to dinner every once in a while.

Yvonne and I tell each other that's how we always want to be. Those people are the coolest. Everyone who breaks up and hates on each other—that's bullshit. We want to be cool with it. No messy divorce-court battles. We stay friends, just like the upstairs-downstairs neighbor couple. We concentrate on our children.

It's a crazy mash-up of a family, but somehow it works. My daughter Lisa is a big part of our lives. I bring her down from Oakland every summer to live with me. I also get to know my oldest sons, Daryl and Duane, much better than I ever did before. They are living in Los Angeles now, so I see them fairly often. One time, I bring the star of one of their favorite horror films, the rat-based fright flick, *Willard,* up to their bedroom to wish them good night. When they see Willard himself, the actor Bruce Davison, come into the room, they freak out.

The other kids are all crazy about the youngest member of the brood, Symeon, the last child Yvonne and I have before we break up. Symeon looks more like Yvonne, while Shane and Spring look like me. Symeon, like Symeon the Righteous from the Bible. The other kids always make a big deal of him, he's their little pet.

One evening we're out as a family at El Coyote, the famous Mexican restaurant in Hollywood. Five-year-old Symeon solemnly checks out the patio, which is dominated by gay males, laughing and drinking. He turns to me.

"Daddy, where are all the mommies?" The whole family cracks up laughing. Out of the mouth of babes.

All the kids have their daddy's show business blood in their veins. Duane and Daryl are already making noise that they want to follow their old man into comedy. Right around this time, Shane lands a role in the second-generation *Roots* series, making his family proud.

This is the hardest period of my friendship with Richard. He goes all scattered and remote on me. Finally, he tells me what's up with him. The tingly feeling he has in his limbs, which we always wrote off as nerve damage from the fire, winds up being the first signs of multiple sclerosis. The dreaded

MS. A disease that slowly attacks the nerve cells in your brain and spinal cord, so that you get more and more messed up, until you can't breathe, can't talk, can't live. There's no cure.

MS happens at different rates for different people, and Richard is convinced he will have the slow kind. He's got healthy years ahead of him, he tells me. It doesn't work out that way. From the middle of the 1980s onward, MS steals a little more from Richard, week by week, month by month. If I don't see him for a little while, and then I go up to Northridge, I am always shocked by the change. My best friend is falling apart right in front of my eyes.

"MS is a motherfucker, Mr. Mooney," he says. "I wouldn't wish it on Annette Funicello." There are rumors back then that the *Beach Blanket Bingo* actress has MS, too.

"I know why God gave me MS," Richard says. "I was a bad guy. I was into drugs. But how could God give it to Annette Funicello? She never did nothing bad. She's a Mouseketeer! I mean, come on, God!"

As Richard is fading, other comics are coming up who idolize him. I first meet Eddie Murphy in New York in 1985, on the set of Richard's movie *Brewster's Millions*. Eddie's been on *Saturday Night Live* since the early 1980s. By the time I meet him, he has already broken out as a big movie star in *48 Hrs.*, *Trading Places*, and *Beverly Hills Cop*. He comes onto the set as a guest of Richard's costar on *Brewster's*, John Candy.

Richard and Eddie huddle up right away. Eddie is telling him how he's been following Richard's every move since he was a little kid on Long Island. John Candy looks over to them and frets. He's jealous of their instant friendship.

"Richard hates me," Candy says.

"Richard doesn't hate you," I say to him, although I know for a fact that Richard cannot stand the man. It's Chevy Chase all over again.

"He never talks to me like that," Candy says, looking over at Eddie and Richard together.

"You ain't black," I say to him, giving him a blinding glimpse of the obvious. I make some excuse and leave the needy fat man to himself.

I occasionally feel resentment from my professional contacts because of my closeness with Richard. Eddie Murphy and I talk about it. "I have Caesar's ear, and they don't like that," I say. I'm one of the few people who can go up and see Richard whenever, wherever.

"I know that I used to hate you," Eddie says. "I was always seeing you with stars, and I got mad at you."

"People dislike you when you have Caesar's ear. They can't get to the king, so they get pissed at you."

Later on, Richard asks me about Murphy. "You don't like him," he says.

"What's there to like?" I say. "He's just a kid." I harbor a secret grudge because I feel as though Eddie has lifted some of my material, or at least did some shit that was similar to mine. Comics always feel that way whether justified or not. It's a chronic condition with us.

I wonder if all alpha males hate on one another at the start. Richard and I don't get along the first time we meet, either, when he tries to lay that orgy shit on me. It takes a while. Same with Eddie. But we go on to become real friends.

"Now Mr. Mooney can get his money from Eddie," Richard says. He says it sort of mock bitterly, like he's half-hurt and half-relieved that I don't have to rely on his broke-down ass for employment.

Meanwhile, Eddie has a beef with Keenan Wayans, another comic who is coming up just then. Keenan gets into Eddie's shit over some material each of them claims as his own. They talk about suing each other. I step in between them.

"Don't do it," I tell Eddie and Keenan both. "It's black-on-black crime, brothers. Black people fighting, you know white people love the shit out of that."

They resolve their differences out of court, and I wind up working with both of them. For his Raw tour in 1987, Eddie invites me to open for him.

I say, "I'm a comic, and you're a comic, and you want me to open for you?"

"That's right," he says.

Keepin' it Raw: Me with Eddie Murphy and his wife, Nicole Mitchell Murphy

It's never been done before. The hard-and-fast showbiz tradition is to mix music and comedy. If the headliner is a comic, you open with a musical act. Richard always has Patti LaBelle open for him. Elvis headlines, and he puts Sammy Shore as the first act.

Eddie's on *Oprah,* and she asks him who his favorite comic is. "Paul Mooney," he says. I have to laugh at the look of terror, disgust, and fascination that crosses Oprah's face at that moment. I am always fucking with her in my act.

Eddie and I go out on the nationwide Raw tour, and we kill. I can tell I am keeping him sharp. He calls the tour "Raw" because Bill Cosby gets down on him publicly, calling his language too raw. Eddie definitely doesn't tone it down in response. Somebody counts up the number of times *fuck* is used in the movie version of his Raw act, and it turns out it's the most ever in a film since the Al Pacino gangster flick *Scarface.*

On the tour bus, they nickname me Indian and Vampire because they never see me sleep. "I have to stay awake and watch this white man drive this bus," I tell them. Any time I close my eyes, I get bus-plunge visions. It's all from my experience as an eighth-month fetus in the womb, getting roller-coastered on a road in Shreveport, Louisiana.

When the Wayans brothers get their own show on Fox in 1990, they call it *In Living Color.* Fox is still trying to break the grip of the Big Three networks back then, so it's open to edgier material than NBC, ABC, and CBS. For the show's ensemble, the Wayans hire some people who go on to be stars, like Jim Carrey, David Alan Grier, and Jamie Foxx.

I don't want to come aboard as a staff writer. But the Wayans create the character of Homey D. Clown off a riff of mine. Homey is a children's party clown who performs the job as part of a prison work-release program. He doesn't take any shit from kids or grown-ups. He's the oppressed figure who is comically vocal about his status.

In one sketch, Jim Carrey leads a Boy Scout–style group to a party with Homey.

> *Jim Carrey (as scout leader):* Do you mind if I use a check to pay for this?
>
> *Damon Wayans (as Homey D. Clown):* Oh, you want to pay me with a check, huh? And have me stand in line at some damned bank in a clown outfit, degrading and shaming myself to cash your little peanuts? I don't think so. Homey don't play that.

Damon slurs the line "your little peanuts" so it sounds like "your little penis."

Homey has a motto, which may as well be words to live by for every comedian who doesn't want to play the coon. "Homey may be a clown," Damon says in character more than once, "but he don't make a fool out of himself."

In Living Color is a phenomenon for Fox, delivering the young viewers the network craves. "Homey don't play that" becomes another of my catchphrases to go national. Richard loves the show. We sometimes watch it together at his place in Northridge. It feels as though our pigeons are coming home to roost. The momentum we started on *The Richard Pryor Show* is playing out with Eddie Murphy, the Wayanses, and other comics like Dave Chappelle. At the same time that the MS slowly takes away Richard's ability to talk, new voices are coming up.

The black pack: Arsenio Hall, me,
Eddie Murphy, Robert Townsend,
and Keenan Ivory Wayans

CHAPTER 29

In spring 1992, a month after the riot against the Rodney King verdicts burns down half of Los Angeles, I'm in the green room at the Pantages Theater at Hollywood and Vine. One of the promoters of the show approaches me with a request.

"Mr. Mooney," he says, actually wringing his hands like he's in a silent movie—probably *Birth of a Nation,* "could you please not mention race?"

I marvel that there's a person on the face of God's green earth who would have the total lack of sense to say something like that to me. It's like someone coming up and saying, "Could you please not breathe?" Who does this imbecile think I am?

I'm not one of those people out there burning down stores or boosting TVs. But I see enough LAPD bullshit in my life to know that this moment is a long time coming. L.A. police are the worst in the world. They're outnumbered, and they know it, so they have to act all heavy-handed to make their presence known.

Richard rents a house in Bel Air to get away from the Northridge craziness. We go up there to work. I leave the house late one night, but the streets are like a maze up there. I'm driving around lost for fifteen minutes. I see a car full of white people, and I think they're lost, too. They trail me for a little while. I finally make it down to Sunset and turn east. I approach the dogleg at the start of the Strip, right where Tower Records is back then, and there's a police roadblock waiting for me.

What the shit is this?

"Some citizen called it in," the cop tells me as he's checking my ID.

"Some citizen? What am I? I'm a citizen. What do you think I am, a baseball bat?"

This is a total no-no in LAPD copland. No back talk, and no black talk. The police will wear a black person out.

"Are you on probation or parole?"

"What?"

"Don't be offended. We ask everybody that. Does the owner of the car know that you have it?"

"What? I'm the owner of this car!"

"Where are you going?"

This bullshit is annoying me. "I'm going to drive until I run out of gas. You want to follow me?"

He gives me the stink-eye and tells me to drive off. There are two LAPD rules that every black second-class citizen of Los Angeles knows. One: you mouth off, you get run in. Two: you flee from a cop, you get a beatdown. That's what happened to Rodney. He got beat because he ran. He broke the unwritten rule of the LAPD.

I've been at a traffic stop in Beverly Hills where the cop reaches across the driver and another passenger, both women, to ask me for my ID. Just me, not the two white women I'm with—and I'm not even driving. I've been hauled out of a store in Hollywood in manacles, taken to the station house, and then told it is all a big mistake. No apologies, no nothing, just a curt, "You're free to go."

"I'm free to go? Then take me back to the store in handcuffs, uncuff me in front of everybody and apologize! You handcuffed me in public, now make it right in public, too!"

No back talk, Negro.

Yes, it might be all new to you, but it's real old for me. For white people, watching the Rodney King video is like a world premiere movie. "Oh, I didn't know the nice policemen did *that*." For black people, it's a rerun. It's been in syndication for a long time. We've seen it all before.

After the King verdict, Richard and I meet up at the Bel Air rental house to watch the fires downtown and in Pico-Union. I think about *The Crazy World of Arthur Brown*: "I'll take you to burn, burn, burn, burn, burn!" And of the slogan during the riots of the 1960s: "Burn, baby, burn!" Yes, we've seen it all before. You can only put pressure on people for so long before they explode.

A month later, at the Pantages that night, the nervous promoter practically follows me onstage. "So will you please not mention race? Please? Mr. Mooney?"

I go out and check the crowd. Black people and brave white people—my kind of audience.

"They don't want me to talk about race!" The first words out of my mouth.

The audience members scream. They *scream*!

"You all got matches? Here, I got some, if you don't have any." I toss out a half-dozen books of matches to the crowd.

They scream. They *scream*!

Who says you can't yell "Fire!" in a crowded theater?

I'm just keeping it real. And my kind of audience likes it real.

Back then, I'm living with a white girl, Lori Petty, the actress. Keanu Reeves's surfer girl in *Point Break*. Kit Keller, Geena Davis's character's little sister, in *A League of Their Own*. Tank Girl. Lori's the coolest. During the riots, she's quoting George Clinton of Parliament Funkadelic—"Let's go downtown and blow the roof off of this sucker!"

Lori and I are together for five good years, until we fall out on the set of a movie we're both acting in, a Pauly Shore comedy called *In the Army Now*. That film kills more than our relationship. Mitzi's son Pauly sees his career pretty much left for dead after it, too.

I am too busy to notice whether or not my film career is tanking. I finally come out with my first album, *Race*. It's good timing, right after the riots. I do a lot of my stand-up routines that feature the same upside-down view of the world that I learn back in childhood, from the "Mama getting her ass whupped" story that makes me laugh so hard.

A lot of times, I just take a black situation and turn it upside down by putting white people in it. The most popular singing group in the country back then is from a goddamned TV commercial (ain't America great?). The California Raisins. The cartoon dried fruit sing "I Heard It Through the Grapevine" with Jimi Hendrix's old drummer, Buddy Miles, on vocals. On my album *Race*, I go off on the whole California Raisin phenomenon.

White folks' favorite TV commercial is that you got to be a little shriveled-up wrinkled black raisin. Little nigger raisin with a hat, they think that shit is cute. [White folk voice] "Oh, look at the cute nigger raisin!" . . . They've gone nigger-raisin crazy. They made Ray Charles . . . and Michael Jackson goddamned raisins . . . They've gone nigger-fucking-raisin crazy. And the shit ain't cute. I bet

*if I get me some goddamned marshmallows, and put some
arms and legs on the goddamned marshmallows, and let
'em sing "Surfin' U.S.A.," they won't think that shit is so
goddamned cute! No, it won't be cute then! White people
will call up and bitch and shit. "I'm not a goddamned
marshmallow! What kind of crazy nigger wrote this commercial?"*

Take a situation, turn it upside down, like you're in a bus
plunge or you're an ass-whupper getting ass-whupped.
Sometimes to go upside down, all I have to do is keep it real,
saying stuff that no one else is saying.

*Because I'm recording, I want to say some good things
about white people. Because sometimes white people
freak out when they see me. [White folk voice] "He hates
us! He doesn't like us!" I don't hate you—I hate your
parents for having you. [White folk voice] "It's a chip on
his shoulder. He's bitter." You folks have names for niggers. White people will label people. You're dirty when it
comes to labeling. 'Cause it will last for years. "The only
good Indian is a dead one." Ain't that a bitch? "The one
thing I hate more than a nigger"—which you can't imagine what—"is a nigger lover." It's true, white folks know
how to label you. They fuck white girls up. "Once you go
black, you won't come back." Come back from where?
What, do they fall into some deep black hole?*

Two-thirds of the way through the album, I get down to
it, trashing the whole idea of black and white labels.

You know that Spike Lee movie? What's that, Jungle
Fever? *All that is bullshit. I'll tell you why. There's no*

such thing as jungle fever. The white man saw to it that everyone is mixed. Blame it on the white man . . . Because he did a lot of fucking, okay? . . . Ain't no "jungle fever," we're too mixed up. Don't let them run that, they're four-hundred-and-fifty years too late for jungle fever. [White folk voice] "Oh, it's all true, we're all God's children." No, we're all black. Everybody is. It's the truth, it's cold, ain't it? But it's real. People in America—because black is negative in the Western world—you can't get them to admit it. They'll admit they got any blood but black. They'll admit their mama is anything but black. "Isn't your mama a goat?" [nodding] "Sure she is—that's why we call her 'Nana'!" Isn't your cousin black? [screams]

Tell me that ain't keeping it real. The *Race* album just takes what I've been saying onstage in my stand-up act and bottles it. For some people, it's poison, but for other people, it's tonic. I know for a lot of white people, it's a fucking relief to get this shit out in the open. *Race* earns me my first Grammy nomination.

Keenan Wayans plays the album to his writers on *In Living Color.* "This is the kind of jokes I want," he tells them. "I want Mooney funny."

The whole country must like it, because for my next album, America gives me the greatest gift anybody has ever given a comic.

O.J.

CHAPTER 30

There's a time when every black person I see looks like O.J. to me. It's the one period when I can say we all look alike. Let me bring you back to the mid-1990s: TV is all O.J., all the time. Same with newspapers and magazines. I spend months O.J.'d out. The coverage bumps *Oprah,* it bumps the soap operas. It's a modern-day *Othello.*

I see that white Bronco on the freeway on TV, and I'm screaming "Run, run, *run!*" Because all black men know that if they're chasing one of us, they're chasing all of us. He has the gun up to his head, I'm saying, "Please don't kill us!" Just like Black Bart in *Blazing Saddles.* When O.J. finally turns himself in, I can finally get some sleep, because I'm not up all night waiting for the LAPD storm troopers to kick in my door.

Like I say, I may have been born yesterday, but I stayed up all night. I may not know anything about complex shit like the space program, but I do know one thing that's pretty damned simple.

O.J. ain't did that. He ain't did what they say he did. That boy ain't did that. No murder weapon, no eye-witness. He's not guilty in a court of law.

White folks just want to play blame-a-nigger. Blame a nigger, any nigger. He kills two people and still catches the red-eye? He wasn't that quick even on the football field. He ran like any good black man will run. We know our history. If the police come through the door with a simple traffic ticket, I know what can happen, and I'd run, too. Any brother will run if he has any sense.

O.J. is under that illusion of inclusion—he ain't been black since he is seventeen years old. He's the only black man in America who can get on any golf course, any time. White America loves that boy.

But he finally gets what I always describe as "the nigger wake-up call." We all get it. Michael Jackson gets it when cops bust into his Neverland Ranch and search his bedroom. Oprah gets her nigger wake-up call when she is closed out of that upscale store in Paris. (I blame her. You can't recognize that woman as being Oprah without makeup. If she doesn't have her hair done and her makeup on, I wouldn't let the woman in my own backyard.)

O.J. finds out but quick that he ain't white, that he's a nigger after all. If he wasn't on camera in the Bronco, they would have found him dead somewhere. The coroner would solemnly testify that he'd broken his neck somehow. Where are all his solid white friends when he is on the run? He has to get his black friend Al to drive him in that Bronco. He has to go back to the ghetto and find someone to help him out, his black friend, his diaper buddy who he grew up with. A nigger wake-up call is the fastest way to see your white friends vanish.

I see O.J. and Al Cowlings in that Bronco and I have to ask myself: if I am accused of a double ax murder, who can I ask to give me a ride? How about if someone else who is accused of a double ax murder comes to my house and asks me to drive them? Ask yourself. Is there anyone I would do that for?

In that situation, I *might* drive Richard around. I might. We're that tight. I am with him after he shoots up Deborah's Buick. I am with him when he's lying in the burn center. But if he kills someone? I don't know if I could drive with him. In fact, I don't know if Mama came around that I would go with her. "Here, Mama, here are the car keys. I love you, Mama. Call me when you get to Mexico. See you on *Hard Copy*."

It's times like these that I miss my friend Richard. He's still around, but he's gone. The MS has already taken him. He can't talk much now, can't form words, can't use sign language. I would go up to his house, and I would talk about O.J., trying to get Richard to laugh.

"Just in case he did do it, I'm sending my résumé to Hertz."

Richard laughs, but his laughter immediately turns into a horrible bout of coughing and hacking. When he finally quits, his mouth hangs open, slack and round, like he's in shock or something. It's awful to see. When I leave him, I'm grieving.

O.J. is exactly the kind of thing we'd crack up over, because it lays bare the kind of race shit that America usually keeps so well hidden. It's that old complexion for the protection bullshit. White people have it, and that means they have the luxury not to think about race except when it suits them. I see a white homeless person on the street, acting the bum in downtown L.A. or somewhere, and I think, *What a waste of a white skin*. He could use that skin for protection, and instead, he's throwing it all away.

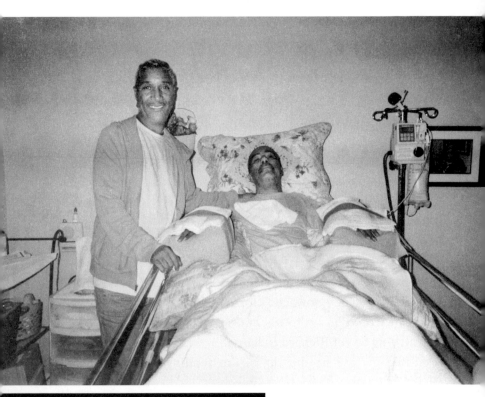

Friends to the end: Me with Richard in the last days before MS takes him

It's during the O.J. trial that I start to feel how alone I really am. I've broken up with Lori. Richard is gone without being gone. I turn more and more to my children.

I do another album, *Master Piece*. O.J. is front and center, race is front and center. It is a bad time for black people in America. There are nigger wake-up calls being placed right and left. The fucking mayor of Washington, D.C., Marion Barry, kicks it off by being caught on tape smoking crack. James Brown, Michael Jackson, Mike Tyson, O.J. They all get their wake-up calls. I lay it all out on *Master Piece,* and sometimes I flip it over and do it upside down, too.

> *Michael Jackson went out and married Elvis's daughter? Go, Michael, go! Elvis Presley's daughter? I was celebrating. I was getting naked and pouring champagne over myself. Yes, yes, yes! I love you! Elvis Presley's daughter? Elvis's daughter? Pimped his ass. Elvis Presley stole so much from black people, it's about time he gave us something back!*

I record the album in Harlem. I still keep a house in L.A., but I am spending more and more time in the city. I like it there, because they like being black in New York. They're very comfortable and not in denial. It's not Hollywood—it's the neighborhood. It's where I feel safe.

I play *Master Piece* for Richard. He doesn't get out to the clubs anymore, so all the material is pretty much new to him. He listens, and when I look into his eyes, they glitter and smile. I know he is getting it. But he can't communicate what he's feeling. He can't express himself. There's good days when he can whisper out a few words, and bad days like this one, when he's mute, locked into silence by the disease. Richard lives to connect, convey, communicate. That's when I know the truth: MS is the last demon he'll ever face. Richard Pryor is in hell.

BLACK

CHAPTER 31

In 2001, my darling youngest son, Symeon, is murdered. It's a mean, ugly death. He's shot from close range in a car parked in an alleyway in L.A. The kid who shoots him, somebody he knows and hangs out with, later drives to Las Vegas, checks himself into a hotel, and commits suicide.

I'm in New York when it happens, and my close friend Eric calls me and tells me that Symeon is gone. My son is in the police station morgue for hours before he is identified. All the morgue knows is that it is holding the body of someone with the last name of Mooney. At first the news organizations think it's me who has died. My close friend, the actor Glynn Turman, sets the situation straight at the morgue.

Symeon is always the kind of child who makes things hard on himself. He even whistles backward. In his late adolescence, he falls in with Ramone, the son of my cousin Raquel. Symeon and Ramone add up to a bad combination. The streets kill my son and send Ramone to prison.

RIP: My son Symeon, who died tragically

When a child of yours dies, you join a very exclusive club. Your children are supposed to outlive you. That's the natural order of things. The only ones who really understand are those who have had this particular tragedy befall them. It's pure torture. The whole family is emotionally wrecked by it. I am only glad that Mama, my dear Mama, is gone so she doesn't have to feel the pain. She passes away the year before in Oakland, and I am at her bedside.

Suddenly it seems I am surrounded by death. Nothing

feels funny anymore. It's the most difficult time in my comedy career. I have to work, I have to support my family. But I feel as though I am two separate people. Mooney at the microphone, and Mooney who has to live his life in grief.

It takes me a long period before I am back on my feet professionally. When Dave Chappelle creates a new sketch comedy TV show on Comedy Central in 2003, I recognize what it is right away. It's got an informal, just-friends-hanging-out-at-a-party vibe and a familiar edge to it. *Chappelle's Show* is done as if *Playboy After Dark* collides with *The Richard Pryor Show*.

One way to tell that someone is good is when Hollywood doesn't know what to do with them. For years, I run into Dave Chappelle on the stand-up scene around the clubs and I see how funny he is. He comes into the Store and asks if he can do a set in front of my audience. When we talk, I always like him personally. I meet his mom, Yvonne, and really like her. Dave is raised in a middle-class household in Washington, D.C., with his father and mother both college professors.

So of course a smart, funny black man like that has trouble finding his place in Hollywood. He turns down the role of Bubba in the movie *Forrest Gump* because he sees the demeaning bullshit behind the character's shuck-and-jive smile. He gets his own sitcom, *Buddies*, a spin-off of an appearance on *Home Improvement*, Tim Allen's joint, but Dave's show gets cancelled right away.

Dave doesn't come into his own until *Chappelle's Show*, which starts out small on cable but blows up huge on DVD. *In Living Color, Chappelle's Show*, they all come from *The Richard Pryor Show*. They grow from it. That ain't an insult. It's a natural thing.

When he sees *Chappelle's Show*, Richard talks about

"passing the torch" to Dave, which considering his relationship with torches and fire, is pretty funny. He's not threatened by Dave, and neither am I. The mothership isn't threatened by all the other ships coming up to it to suck teat.

Dave puts together an ensemble that includes Charlie Murphy (Eddie's brother), Bill Burr, and Donnell Rawlings. Dave asks me to write for *Chappelle's Show* and I lay out my conditions for him right away. "I've been in this business too long," I tell him. "I can't get into another bullshit situation where I have producers and executives picking apart my shit."

"I won't let them fuck with your stuff," Dave promises.

It ain't the easiest work in the world, running interference for me with Hollywood people who don't understand comedy and never will, but Dave does it like a pro. But it's like I'm seeing Richard's response to Hollywood playing out in Dave's experience, too. They're both comic geniuses. They're both trying to maneuver through the Hollywood minefield. They both feel stressed out by white people loving their shit so much, as though that means they aren't keeping it real. And they both wind up fleeing Hollywood for Africa. Seeing the way things turn out, I feel bad that I probably added to Dave's stress level. But I can only do what I do.

One thing I like to do is fuck with things that white people consider their own. White folks love them some mysticism. They like funny-ass religions like Buddhism and Scientology because it helps them get out from under the Ten Commandments. They like tarot cards and aliens and all that shit. And they believe in Nostradamus seeing the future. Nostradamus is a French druggist from half a millennium ago, and white people are reading books about him, nodding their heads like he's Dionne Warwick down at the Psychic Friends Network.

White people have Nostradamus, so I give *Chappelle's Show* Negrodamus. We intro the bit with trippy music and random voices asking questions.

What's the meaning of life? Am I going to find a husband? Who is my real father? Does God really exist? [female announcer] *For centuries, people have turned to one man for the answers to life's great mysteries. That man is Negrodamus.*

I come on tricked-out with a burgundy fop hat, a French beard, and a doublet. I field questions from the audience.

Audience member: Negrodamus, what mistakes did Michael Jackson make before he was arrested?
Negrodamus: Michael Jackson should not have been a singer. He should have been a priest. That way, he would have just been transferred.
Audience member: Negrodamus, why is President Bush so sure Iraq has weapons of mass destruction?
Negrodamus: Because he has the receipt.

I also fuck with movie review shows like *Siskel and Ebert,* because none of them ever use a black critic. For "Mooney on Movies," I ask Dave to hire me the "whitest white girls you can get." I have blond actresses on either side of me, playing the kind of women whose media-created opinions come out of their mouths totally prefabricated.

White woman #1: Our first film is *Gone With the Wind*. This film is an epic romance centering around Scarlett O'Hara, a damsel in distress during the Civil War. It is a must-see, must-own movie. I highly recommend it.

White woman #2: I couldn't agree with you more. I've actually seen *Gone With the Wind* thirteen times since I was ten years old, no kidding.

Mooney: You must be on crack. I don't think we've seen the same movie. I thought Scarlett was a ho', because she went to bed with everybody but Mammy. I love Mammy. The best scene in the movie is when Mammy told the people, "Get off my porch, white trash." I stood and I applauded. I liked every bit of it.

White woman #2: I liked Mammy. I thought she was great, I thought she had a great role.

Mooney: It was Hattie McDaniels. Do you know in real life they wouldn't let Mammy go to the opening? Hollywood goes too far. She's dead, but everybody comes back to get their money. She came back as Oprah Winfrey.

A couple of things are going on here. I'm playing a role, a movie critic. Even though the title of the bit is "Mooney on Movies," I'm not being me. I'm sending up a TV movie critic such as Roger Ebert. Also, I'm getting at something that has happened to me again and again: a white person and a black person encounter the exact same material, and they come away with opposite reactions to it as different as black and white.

I get more street recognition from Negrodamus and my other characters on *Chapelle's Show* than I have ever gotten before. Even with no advertising push behind it, the program is huge. It sells like ice in hell on DVD, moving more than 3 million copies, becoming the best-selling TV show on DVD ever, ahead of even *The Simpsons*. America is like a thirsty dog at its water bowl. It drinks that shit up. Richard Pryor has been away from the scene too long. But Dave Chappelle gives them the next best funnyman.

As a result of my new high profile, the BET channel folks invite me to appear on their awards show in September 2005. It doesn't turn out well. They hire Mooney, they get Mooney. Maybe they were under the mistaken impression that they had hired Mickey Rooney. I give my Nigger Wake-Up Call Award, with the nominees being Diana Ross, Lil' Kim, Michael Jackson, and Oprah Winfrey.

> *Diana Ross, Diva! They arrest her for DUI, and she says, "Do you know who I am?" They say, "Yeah, you're the bitch who's going to jail!" She's in the jail hallway* [singing "Love's Hangover"], *"If there's a cure for this, I don't want it, don't want it." "Get back in your cell, bitch, and shut up!"*

Diana Ross's daughter Tracee is in the audience that night, and she runs out of the auditorium crying. I get slammed left and right. My bit is almost completely edited out of the broadcast. I never felt the love at BET, which I call "almost black television," because I know it's owned by white folks. But getting fucked with for doing my own comedy is too much. I watch Dave Letterman and Jay Leno every night. They fuck with celebrities and get off scot-free. When folks start calling them down, start criticizing them, then they can start in on me. Until then, don't bother me. I've got shows to do.

CHAPTER 32

Richard Franklin Lennox Thomas Pryor III, RIP, December 10, 2005.

He was the better part of me.

CHAPTER 33

I know it's coming, but when it happens, I'm still not prepared for Richard's death. Ever since Symeon is murdered, I have a sense of foreboding. The last years of Richard's life are so painful to watch that I feel guilty for wishing the good Lord would just take him to rest. MS is pure evil. It breaks a man down into a baby again.

I find it hard to keep the real Richard in my mind the way I want to remember him, laughing during a roast on *The Richard Pryor Show,* hanging out at Redd Foxx's club, singing Motown at the top of our lungs on the drive north from L.A. to Berkeley.

Fuck the world. Fuck the world for being poorer without Richard Pryor in it.

Things keep happening that I want Richard to see, that I want Richard to react to. I am doing a *Showtime at the Apollo* episode when they actually stop the whole shit and censor my ass offstage. "Hey, Richard," I say to his memory, "this ain't the old Apollo that we know." The theater is owned by Time Warner now, and they don't like me criticizing a sitting president. It might interfere with their lobbying efforts in Washington.

Fuck the Bushes. I hate the whole family. Like that mother of his, she looks like the guy on the Quaker Oats box . . .

They pull my ass right off the stage. The whole show stops for a motherfucking hour over that shit. "What happened?" I keep asking. "You offended an executive from Time Warner," somebody tells me. "What? Who?" I never get a straight answer, and I resolve never to play the Apollo again until I am satisfied.

After the dust settles I have a thought that's going to be with me the rest of my life: *I wish Richard were here to see this shit.* I want to call him. We would laugh about the bullshit the way we always do.

I have the same thought when Michael Richards goes berserk onstage at the Laugh Factory in West Hollywood. He's pissed because of some loud audience members. First he says, "Look at the stupid Mexicans and blacks being loud up there." Then he derails completely.

Richards: Shut up! Fifty years ago we'd have you upside down with a fucking fork up your ass! You can talk, you can talk, you can talk, you're brave now, motherfucker. Throw his ass out! He's a nigger! He's a nigger! He's a nigger!
Female audience member: Oh my god.
Richards: A nigger! Look, there's a nigger!
[*Audience gasps audibly.*]
Richards: What's the matter? Is this too much for you to handle? They're going to arrest me for calling a

black man a nigger? [*off the audience member leaving*] Wait a minute—where's he going?

Audience member, leaving: That was uncalled-for, you fucking cracker-ass motherfucker.

Richards: Cracker-ass? You calling me cracker-ass, nigger?

Audience member, leaving: We've had it. We've had it.

Richards: That's what happens when you interrupt the white man, don't you know?

Yeah, Michael, we know. Listening to the exchange, I'm sucked right back to 1975 on *Saturday Night Live,* with Richard and Chevy Chase going at it in my word-association job-interview routine.

Cheap motherfucker!

Fucking white boy!

Nigger!

Cracker-ass!

Thirty-one years later, it's still going down in real life. I've known Michael Richards for a long time. I see him around the clubs in the late 1970s and all through the 1980s. He is friendly and never strikes me as racist. But scratch a white man and you'll hear a bigot scream.

Seeing Michael Richards reveal his inner racist makes me reconsider my own use of the word. Richard gives up the *N* word in his act after a trip to Africa in spring 1979. "You know, Mooney, I looked all around in Kenya, and you know what? I didn't see no niggers. I was sitting in the lobby in the hotel in Nairobi, and a voice inside me asks, 'What do you see?' I see all kinds of people. 'Do you see any niggers?' No, I don't see any niggers. And I started crying, Paul. Right there in the lobby."

Richard has always been an old softie. So he stops using the word onstage. I don't. I figure I've been called "nigger" so many times, I can damn well use it whenever I want. But it starts to die in my mouth a little bit when I see all the comics and rappers coming up, using it like a crutch.

Some people try to run a game that *nigger* and *nigga* are two different words. That one is okay, the other one isn't. But I know that if you spell it with an *-er* or an *-a,* it's all the same. It's as though flinging the word *nigger* around is all they take from Richard and me, as though that's all we are. They don't get it.

When Michael Richards runs that shit, I figure it's time. Michael calls me up and asks me what the fuck he should do. I tell him he has to face up to it. I go on a CNN show about the incident and announce that I am giving up the word onstage. "Instead of 'What's up, my nigger,' I'm going to say, 'What's up, my Michael Richards.'"

Jesse Jackson and Reverend Al Sharpton summon me to a summit with Michael at the Hollywood Hilton. Michael is beside himself. He doesn't know if I was going to hit him or hug him.

"Help me, Paul," he pleads. "I got crazy people calling me up, telling me how much they agree with me! I don't want to be Ku Klux Klan!"

At the meeting, I forgive Michael. I'm sincere. I figure he's been away from stand-up too long, acting the fool on *Seinfeld.* Stand-up is unforgiving. You can't go away from it. You lose your edge. It's like Jesse James putting up his guns. You can't just jump back into it. You'll get killed.

CHAPTER 34

Flash forward to the end of October 2008, to my appearance on *The Late Show with David Letterman*. The whole country is swept up in presidential-election fever. Barack Obama is leading John McCain in the polls.

I'm totally tripping when Dave invites me to the couch. I'm giving voice to what I'm hearing in the streets. I know Obama is going to win.

"Obama beats your mama!" I laugh, yelling it out. "Obama beats your mama!"

A cry of victory, over and over. Dave can't control me.

The next day I get a call from *Superman*'s Lois Lane, the actress Margot Kidder, who is one of Richard's old girl-friends. I know her from way back, but she hasn't talked to me in years. Suddenly she's on the phone.

"How can you say that, Paul?" she says, launching right in.

"What? Who is this?"

"You're going to stop them from voting for Obama," Kidder says.

After my initial shock, I finally get it straight in my mind. Here's this actress, long-ago friend, she gets brain-lock over the fact that Obama might not win, and she's freaking out. She wants me to tone it down. She wants me to act nice and quiet and not rock the boat.

Honey, I am born rocking the boat. I don't even have to do a thing in order to rock the boat. I don't have to stand up and swivel my hips like Elvis did. Just me, just me being who I am, rocks the damn boat.

I ask Margot Kidder how she can tell me not to be who I am. I'm a performer. I'm on David Letterman's show, doing my act. And you're this Lois Lane lady who somehow thinks it's okay to try to shush me up? You're telling me about comedy?

After all this time, I've learned that people's reactions to me often have nothing to do with me. Any of the hundreds of executives who I've run up against in Hollywood: It's their trip, it's not mine.

It's about color. That's what up. It's not complicated. It's not some paradox. It's simple, it's basic, it's racial. Because that's their problem. Their problem is with the black male. It's true all over the world. Because we're the shit, okay? The American black male is the shit.

I am not intending any disrespect to Africans. I know what the game is. But the American black man is a unique kind of black person. All over the world, people copy us. Our music, the way we talk, the way we walk, they are all influenced by us. We are the most imitated people on earth.

So how does that work out to disrespecting us? Because human beings always have a love-hate relationship with those in power. The black American male has so much power because he is the world's coolest icon. People love us for it, and they hate us for it, too. Everybody wants to be a nigger, but nobody wants to be a nigger. It's complicated that way.

Somehow I become the spokesperson for all this. Whoopi calls me up, and she's only half kidding, but she asks for special dispensation so she can use the word *nigger* that weekend.

"Paul, I got some people coming over, and I know I am going to need to call them some nigger-ass motherfuckers. I just need a pass for this one weekend, so I can use the *N* word, just this once. You give me a pass, Mooney?"

I'm laughing, and I give her the pass. I remember how much trouble she got into when she and her boyfriend at the time, Ted Danson, do a Friars Club roast in blackface. Ted Danson is a black man for one night, and look how much shit it brings him.

I call her up after the Friar's roast. "Welcome to the club," I say. I defend her on the talk shows. If they hate on Whoopi, they have to hate on everyone else who ever appears in blackface. They have to hate on Al Jolson, Frank Sinatra, Lucille Ball, Red Skelton, and Mickey Rooney, because they all wore blackface at one time or another.

I'm on Geraldo's show about the Friars Club beef, and I ask him to come back to me once at the end of the program to say good night. Then I slip off to makeup. When the camera finds me at the end, I'm in whiteface. Geraldo drops the mic, he's laughing so hard. But the bit is censored out of the show.

It's like the joke about a white woman who bakes a chocolate cake. Her little eight-year-old son grabs some of the chocolate frosting, rubs it all over his face, and says, "Look, mama, I'm black."

Mama slaps the shit out of him. "Damn, boy, don't do anything like that ever again! In fact, go in to your father and tell him what you just did!"

The boy goes in to his father, and his father gives him an ass-whupping. The father tells him to go see his grandfather for some discipline. The grandfather wails into him, too.

He goes back to his mama, all hangdog, his ass hurting like a motherfucker.

His mama asks, "Now, sonny, what have you learned?"

"I learned I've been a black person for only five minutes, and already I hate you white people."

CHAPTER 35

I write a lot of this book-joint shit in Magic Johnson's Starbucks on 125th Street in Harlem. Magic Johnson owns half the town up here. He used to be a poster child for AIDS. Now people are running around asking, Where can I get some of that AIDS that Magic has? It's commercial-success AIDS! I want my own Starbucks! I want my own movie theater!

Across the street from Magic Johnson's Starbucks is the old Hotel Theresa, which used to be the only luxury hotel in Manhattan open to black folks. Hotel Theresa is where Fidel Castro stays when he comes to New York City in the 1960s, to make the point that he doesn't want to be downtown with all the white capitalist folks. Across the street is the Adam Clayton Powell State Office Building, where Bill Clinton has his offices ever since he left the White House.

Just like Fidel and Bill, I prefer uptown, too. I live in Harlem, with all the white people. There are more white people in Harlem now than there are in Vermont. Even though they buy apartments and town houses and condos uptown like no mortgage crisis is happening, you never hear them admit that they live in Harlem.

Where do you live?

"I live in Harlem Heights." "Morningside Heights." "Hamilton Heights." All these *heights*. So they can look down on folks.

Where do you live?

"I live in North Manhattan."

North Manhattan? What the hell is that?

How about that big old Harlem roach over there, what do you think of that? "Oh, that's not a roach. That's a water bug." For the white people up here, the rats are raccoons, the silverfish are dachshunds, and the black people are their friends. There is some serious denial going on. They are floating down that river in Egypt.

White people moving into Harlem are crowding out the rats. It's serious. Rats up here are big. They walk upright. They smoke cigarettes. Look at 'em wrong, they'll get on your jock like werewolves. They're huge, and they can climb buildings. They're ninja rats.

Early on during my visits to the city from the West Coast, I find out all about New York rats. I come to Manhattan one time and Columbia Pictures puts me up in a Midtown hotel. They give me a big suite because we have a film deal in the works. I look out the window, and I see a big old ninja rat staring back at me. We're twenty-five floors up, how did that rat get there?

I'm on the phone to the front desk, shouting, "Call the health department—there's a rat up here!" At the same time, the ninja rat is on his phone, calling the police department. "There's a black man up here in a giant hotel suite, he must be robbing the place!"

So a few years ago when I move to New York and find a

space, it ain't a suite at no Midtown hotel. I go uptown and rent a nice apartment in a Harlem brownstone. Only thing is, every time my landlord sees me on TV, he raises my rent. What's that about, you profiteer asshole? You didn't care what I did before, when I wasn't doing anything, why do you care now?

I know my history. Harlem begins as a real estate boondoggle. White developers build it. But they have too many apartments, and nobody to rent them. Then a recession comes. The only people who want the Harlem apartments are black people moving up from the South. I still see some graffiti in Harlem: LANDLORDS AREN'T LORDS OF THE LAND, THEY'RE SCUM OF THE EARTH.

Harlem is where I meet the man who'll become the next president of the United States. Across Lenox, I see Al Sharpton come out of Sylvia's Restaurant with Barack Obama.

A week before this, I'm at Reverend Al's birthday party. October 2007. Al Sharpton, who is related to Strom Thurmond through their great-great slaveholding grandfather. Ain't America superb? Ain't it the shit?

Al says the party is for his fifty-second birthday. Please. He's fifty-two? Reverend Al's *hairdo* is fifty-two years old. But I'm at his birthday party. He keeps calling this Asian girl "Lil' Kim." I think, Reverend Al's gone insane. Why's he calling this little Asian girl Lil' Kim? That's not Lil' Kim!

She turns to me and smiles and I run away. Over to the other side of the party. But she follows me. I turn around, and I realize, holy shit, it *is* Lil' Kim. Girl has had so much plastic surgery she turned Asian? Reverend Al laughs like a madman at my confusion.

"Paul Mooney!" Yelling across Lenox Avenue at me now, from in front of Sylvia's. I walk on down the street like I don't want to go over and say hello. Reverend Al's going to dog me out for not recognizing Lil' Kim-che. I know it.

"Paul Mooney!"

But then I realize it's not Reverend Al calling me after all. It's Barack Obama.

Barack Obama knows me? I'm floored. Or because I'm out on the street, I'm pavemented. Never met him before, never had any dealings with the man.

So I cross the street.

He's just Senator Barack Obama then. Hasn't won any primaries yet or nothing. But he's announced, so he's got a whole platoon of security with him and Reverend Al. He's got Secret Service, FBI, CIA, National Guard, SWAT, he's got Boy Scouts and Jesus Christ with him.

"Paul Mooney!" Obama says. "All the stars are out tonight." He's in a suit and looking like a *GQ* model.

Reverend Al stands there preening, like he's so happy to put us two together, even though it is none of his doing.

"You going to the Apollo?" Al says.

Some event is happening at the landmark theater around the corner. I tell him no, I'm not going to the Apollo. Right then I don't say I'm boycotting the place since Time Warner censored me there. Not the time or the place to get into that shit.

Obama puts out his hand to shake but I shake my head no at him.

"Don't give me that white man's handshake," I say.

I hold out my fist. *This is how you do it*. He doesn't know what to do at first. How to handle it.

On the campaign, people shake hands so much, they get maimed. The Republican wife lady, the pill popper, what's her name? Cindy McCain. Broke her hand. Clinton and those people, they know not to wear any big rings. The public will crush their hands. Democracy.

Obama tightens his hand into a fist. He jabs the air, we

miss. Finally, he gets it right. We bump fists. From then on, he's unstoppable, a crazy fist-bumping Barack-and-roll candidate, doesn't want any more crushed hands.

Half a year later, in summer 2008, during the election campaign, all hell breaks loose because Obama and Michelle fist bump and white people freak out. Suddenly, the two of them are terrorists. Bad enough his middle name, now he's doing that jihadi fist jab.

I kept my head down over that shit. I didn't want people to say, you taught Obama the fist bump, Mooney, now we got that Arizona Mr. Whiteman in the White House.

If I have to explain, I usually tell people I don't shake hands because of germs, like that bald, strikebreaking, briefcase-carrying, game-show comic Howie Mandel. Totally germaphobic. He used to wear gloves to protect himself from microbes.

Germs ain't it. Or they ain't all of it. Know your history. Handshaking means, *I don't have a weapon in my hand.* That's how it started, to keep people from getting medieval on each other's asses.

The hell with that. I don't want nobody to know nothing about my shit. I don't want them to know whether or not I got a weapon. People I run into sometimes, yeah, they *need* to think I got a ministiletto curled up inside my hand, that's right, or a tiny Abraham Lincoln–killing-style derringer, or some pepper-spray shit, you know what I mean?

Fist bump, now. Don't give me no white man's handshake. *Fist bump!*

CHAPTER 36

Harlem is haunted. I ain't talking about no Harlem Renaissance shit, Langston Hughes and W. E. B. DuBois and all those black-history-month folks. I always tell kids if they ever want to do a real report for black-history month, they should hand in a paper on Jesus. Write about Jesus Christ. He's black.

But Harlem is haunted because ever since Richard's death, every place in the world is haunted for me. I know Richard starts his career here in New York City, down in the clubs of the Village. He kicks off his comeback after Berkeley at the Apollo Theater in Harlem. So I am walking the streets, minding my own business, and suddenly a thought of Richard blindsides me. It can happen any time at all.

I'm in a Harlem McDonald's, subway coming aboveground right here and shaking its rattletrap ass over my head, and I sit listening to a short crazy dude sound off. All I can think of is Richard, hearing this tight little African leprechaun (an Africaun?) rant and rave in a strange, high-pitched nuts-in-a-vise voice. The dude rants to everybody in the

Harlem McDonald's, but he's not speaking to anybody in particular. He's talking to thin air.

"I beat you and I hit you," this little Africaun says. "You think I'm small, but I can do it. Come at me, let me see you bring it. I win, because you know why? I may have small hands, but I got God in my hand, right here. *God is in my hands.* You don't know? I used to be a great opera singer."

I say, laughing, "Oh, little man, I wish my friend Richard were around."

If Richard were alive now, I'd write him such a great character. I'd give the little Africaun to him and he'd make a million dollars out of doing the character of the little dude with a big-assed rant. I can see it like it is happening right in front of me. I can see Richard doing him. I miss Richard. Mr. Mooney. I miss him calling me that.

Mostly when I think about Richard, I think about keeping it real. I think about never losing my voice, never giving in, never selling out, always keeping black, always sticking to the street. Staying neighborhood and not Hollywood.

I mean, I've been doing what I do for a long time. I've made millions of dollars at it. I've always worked, throughout the course of five decades now. Not many comedians can say that.

Stop a random black person in the street and ask if the name "Paul Mooney" rings a bell. Now stop a random white person. Two different realities. Maybe that's what we're talking about.

I'm unheard-of by white people. I'm stealth for white people. I'm silent to white people.

So after a half century doing comedy, I'm some sort of secret? I'm the real unknown comic, not that Canadian who used to appear with a paper bag over his head on *The Gong Show*. What's his name? Murray Langston. Somebody put a bag over my reputation. I'm known for being unknown.

Or maybe I'm unknowable.

Or maybe some people just don't want to know me.

All my life, I witness reactions to my presence that seem to veer crazily from fascination to denial. Love-hate. But Mama bestows upon me the greatest gift: an absolute bedrock belief in myself. I'm the ugly duckling who right from the start always knows he's a swan. So the people who want me to be a duck just seem silly to me.

"You're different," Mama tells me. "You've got the light shining from within you."

So it's that light, that God-given light, that makes people respond to me in such strange ways.

What I'm wanting to do with this book-joint thing is give you a glimpse behind the curtain. I'm the one operating the special effects and the fireworks and the light show to make the Great and Powerful Oz great and powerful. That's who I am.

Mama's supreme gift means I'm untouchable. Her unconditional love makes me bulletproof. "You are better than anyone," Mama whispers to me. "You don't have to bow and scrape."

So I'm not slowed down or changed by any of the bullshit thrown at me. I always have the same reaction: I just think it's strange.

I'm trying to come up with a comparison. Say there's a single surviving dragon, the last one in all existence. People are fascinated by it, but they're terrified, too. You can imagine all the excited chatter.

"There's only one left?"

"Are you sure?"

"Omigod, I'm *glad* there's only one left."

Then the dragon wakes up and spits out a few fiery words, and the people are shocked and even more fascinated and terrified.

"You mean it can talk?"

I cannot be any other way than how I am. I can't "tone it down." I can't "be less black." I never worry about whether that person gets me or that person doesn't. I've got the endorsement of the world's funniest man in my hip pocket. Richard helps me to keep going. Even from the grave, he insists on my keeping it real.

Dr. King says, "Human salvation lies in the hands of the creatively maladjusted." I am just happy to be of service to the human race, with all my maladjusted creativity in play every day of the week.

The paper for this book is white and the print is black. Are either of those shades even close to the skin colors of white folks and black folks? No. Malcolm has his realization moment, when he looks up *white* and *black* in the dictionary and sees that it's all bullshit. White people take the color white for their own when they ain't white, they're shades of pink and red and tan. And they assign black folk the color black, when we ain't black, we're brown and tan and high yellow and motherfucking russet.

To paraphrase H. Rap Brown, racism is as American as cherry pie. It's the country's original sin—that and the shit the Europeans pull on the Indians, which is part of the same trip. Racism is a thread that runs through history. Everything is stitched with its color.

So let's play a little word association again, shall we?

Brother.

Sister.

Honky.
　　Honkytonk.

Afro.
　　Euro.

African American.
　　European American.

Obama.
　　President.

Nigger.
　　President.

Tar baby.
　　President.

Jungle bunny, motherfucker!
　　President.

Pink.
　　Tan.

Brown.
　　High yellow.

White.
　　Black.

　　That's right. What'd I say? Black is the new white.

June 2008–April 2009
Harlem
Los Angeles

APPENDIX
PAUL MOONEY: STAND-UP, TV, AND MOVIE CREDITS

STAND-UP

Know Your History: Jesus Was Black . . . So Was Cleopatra (2006)

Analyzing White America (2004)

Master Piece (1994)

Race (1993)

TV

Chappelle's Show (2003), writer, actor

In Living Color (1990), writer

Pryor's Place (1984), writer

The Richard Pryor Show (1977), writer, actor

Saturday Night (1975), writer

Good Times (1974), writer

Sanford and Son (1972), writer

MOVIES

Why We Laugh: Black Comedians on Black Comedy (2009), documentary

The Ketchup King (2002), actor
Call Me Claus (2001), writer
PBS Hollywood Presents, "The Old Settler" (2001), actor
Bamboozled (2000), actor
High Freakquency (1998), actor
In the Army Now (1994), actor
The Legend of Dolemite (1994), documentary
Hollywood Shuffle (1987), actor
Jo Jo Dancer, Your Life Is Calling (1986), writer
Bustin' Loose (1981), actor
I Know Why the Caged Bird Sings (1979), actor
The Buddy Holly Story (1978), actor
Which Way Is Up? (1977), actor
F.T.A. (1972), documentary

ACKNOWLEDGMENTS

Some of the names in this book have been changed to protect the guilty. Some of the other names that haven't been changed represent people who have not been charged just yet, have had the benefit of a hung jury or managed to bribe the judge. You all know who you are.

I have to begin by thanking God for a life of unbelievable bounty and love. These gifts were provided to me first and foremost by my grandmother—my beloved Mama—and by my mother and family, especially my children: Daryl, Duane, Lisa, Shane, and Spring. I love you with all my heart. And to absent friends and family, Richard Pryor, Preston Ealy, and Symeon Mooney. You will always be an inspiration in my life.

Thanks go out to Joe Gilbert and Eddie Brown for getting me my first paying comedy job, Dick Stewart for my first taste of fame, Velva Davis and the Miss Bronze Contest, H. B. Barnum, Alan Winkur, Joyce Selznick for *The Buddy Holly Story*, Hugh Hefner for *Playboy After Dark*, Fred Williamson for not putting me in his movies, and Don Cornelius for putting me on *Soul Train*.

A heartfelt thanks to all the people who I have worked with in Hollywood and beyond, among them Natalie Cole, Aretha Franklin, Miles Davis, Carmen McCrae, Chakka Khan, Tina Marie, Tammi Terrell, Marvin Gaye, Jesse Jackson for saving me from Mayor Bradley, Diahann Carroll, Lou Gossett, Calvin Lockhart, Pam Grier, Jane Fonda, Glenn Turman, Lauren Hutton, Rosie Grier, Faye Dunaway, Roseanne Barr, Sandra Bernhard, Johnnie Witherspoon, Flip Wilson, Lily Tomlin, Sammy Davis, Jr., Damon Wayans, Ben Vereen for hiring me to open for him, Connie Stevens, Vicki Carr, Lana Turner, Suzanne Pleshette, Phyllis Diller, Mitzi Shore, Caroline Hearst, Debbie Allen, Arsenio Hall, Don King, George Slaughter, Bert Sheridan, Nina Simone, Grace Jones, Jackie Collins, Moms Mabley, Rudy Ray Moore, Redd Foxx, Nancy Wilson, Lindsay Wagner, Barbi Benton, Janet Pendleton, Barbara Luna, Morgana King, Isaac Hayes, Whoopi Goldberg, Johnny Mathis, James Brown, Little Richard, Gladys Knight and the Pips, Ann-Margaret, Marcia Warfield, and Jim Brown.

And a very special thanks to Keenan Wayans, Robert Townsend, Dave Chappelle, and Eddie Murphy—for all the laughs over the years, yeah, but more than that, for their deep understanding.

I'd like to extend a million thanks to my longtime manager, Helene Shaw, a true friend and the person most responsible for motivating me to do this book. My editor, Tricia Boczkowski at Simon Spotlight Entertainment, has been great to work with. Mary Pelloni and Gil Reavill helped me transform my thoughts and words into a book.

And, always, thanks to the audiences, for giving me the great gift of their laughter.